P9-DIB-751

DOCUMENTS OF MODERN HISTORY

DOCUMENTS OF MODERN HISTORY

SWEDEN AS A GREAT POWER 1611–1697

GOVERNMENT: SOCIETY: FOREIGN POLICY

edited by

Michael Roberts

Professor of Modern History in The Queen's University of Belfast

New York · St. Martin's Press · 1968

First published 1968

First published in Great Britain by
Edward Arnold (Publishers) Ltd

First published in
the United States of America in 1968

Library of Congress Catalog Card Number: 68-29381

Printed in Great Britain by
Robert Cunningham and Sons Ltd, Alva

CONTENTS

B

The Social Crisis

C

Foreign Affairs

PREFACE

To present a really representative collection of documents, covering the major aspects of Sweden's career as a great power, is obviously impossible in a volume of this size. I have chosen therefore to try to illustrate only three main topics; but even with that limitation the difficulty of exclusion and excision has proved formidable: not only have many documents been omitted which might seem obviously entitled to inclusion, but those which have been retained have necessarily been drastically cut, though I hope without impairing or distorting their character. For much wise and fortifying counsel on the use of the pruning-shears I am indebted to my colleague, Dr John Bossy; and to him, as well as to Mrs Anthea Orr, who typed and retyped several versions of the text, I should like to express my grateful thanks. For the translations, which may occasionally be felt to be a little free, I must bear all the responsibility.

Belfast, M. R.
5 June 1967

INTRODUCTION

The following collection of documents attempts to illustrate the progress of Swedish institutions, and the problems of Swedish society, against the background of Sweden's rise and decline as a great power. And though for purposes of convenience the documents are grouped into three sections, those sections are in reality closely interdependent. Social and constitutional consequences flowed from decisions on foreign policy, and in their turn had an influence upon it: the mounting cost of war entailed the financial weakness of the crown, and seemed to threaten the country with social revolution; the impoverishment of the state in its turn debilitated foreign policy; the solution of a major social problem, and the recovery of military efficiency, were bought at the price of the abandonment of constitutional traditions and the temporary blighting of an emergent parliamentarism.

The basic object of Swedish foreign policy between 1611 and 1697 was security: security against the dynastic threat from Warsaw; against an Imperialist control of the southern Baltic coastlands; against the possibility of Danish attack, or Danish blackmail at the Sound. But the attainment of security was an expensive business, involving a constant quest for resources to supplement those which Sweden herself could provide; and that quest gave to Swedish policy the aggressive character which so alarmed contemporary Europe. In the course of the century these supplementary resources were sought in various quarters: in the long-continuing dream of a monopoly-control of the trade between Russia and the West (**XXXI**); in a substantial *satisfactio* in Germany (**XXXIII, XXXVI-XXXVII**); in control of the customs-dues at Prussian ports (**XXXIX**), or in the seizure of the Sound Dues themselves (**XL**). The development of native industry and native shipping, the attempt in the twenties to achieve a virtual monopoly of the copper-market, were other aspects of the same problem. But in fact the problem was never really solved. Even during the great days of the German war, Sweden's military performance was to some extent dependent on French subsidies (**XXXII, XXXVI**(*b*)); and when the period of expansion ended in 1660 Sweden for a generation became of necessity a subsidy-hunting power (**XLII**). The extension of Swedish territory to include great ports such as Riga and Bremen, or lesser ones such as Stralsund and Wismar, no doubt brought economic gains; but they were more than offset by the cost of defending extended frontiers and maintaining a navy strong enough to hold the scattered maritime empire together. By the 1650s, when the very special conditions of the German war were over, it was already true that Sweden could not afford to keep permanently on foot an army adequate to the defence of her territories: if any crisis should blow up which entailed even partial mobilization, that crisis must probably end in war, since the burden of the armed forces could hardly be borne unless a good part of it was transferred to the shoulders of the enemy by the invasion of his territory (**XXXIX**).

Even before that date, the strain of war had begun to have serious effects upon the domestic situation: 'as the branches expand, the tree withers at the roots'. To carry on the struggle in Germany Gustav Adolf and Oxenstierna needed revenues in specie rather than in kind: armies in Germany could not be paid in butter, iron, hides or tar. Their policy was therefore to sell or pawn such revenues for cash, and to rely increasingly upon indirect taxes and customs-dues. Royal revenues were therefore sold for lump sums; which meant that peasants who had formerly paid tax or rent to the crown now paid it to the purchaser, who was usually a noble. It was expected that the loss to the crown in permanent revenue would be made good by the increased yield of indirect taxation which it was believed would follow the more intensive cultivation of land which had passed into noble hands. The event did not justify the expectation; and the crown's financial position deteriorated alarmingly (**XXII–XXVI**). So too, it was feared, did the position of the peasants who now had to pay their taxes to a noble landlord: their title to freehold ownership seemed to be in jeopardy, and they complained of unscrupulous pressures and unprecedented extortions from the nobility who had stepped into the crown's place (**XXI**, **XXIII–XXIV**). The most recent research suggests that their fears were exaggerated, that cases of noble oppression were not very common, and that the courts did provide a remedy (see **XXV**); but what mattered was not so much the actual state of affairs, as what might happen in the future, and what the peasantry believed to be happening at the moment. The nobility as a class certainly did very well out of the German war: it grew enormously both in wealth and numbers; it indulged in massive prestige-spending; it built great houses, and claimed peasant labour-service in their building. Out of this situation (a direct consequence of foreign policy) came the social crisis of 1650, and the demand (which went back at least to the 1590s) for a resumption by the crown of alienated lands and revenues – in short, for a Reduction.

The crisis of 1650, however, was not only social: it had important constitutional implications. In the first half of the seventeenth century, two strands of constitutional development are clearly discernible in Sweden: on the one hand the long-standing tradition of checks upon the arbitrary power of the crown; on the other the vigorous development of parliamentary institutions. The first of these was essentially aristocratic. It looked back to the fifteenth century, when the monarchy had still been elective; its great protagonist was the Council of the Realm; its principles were embodied in the King's coronation-oath. It had won a resounding victory in Gustav Adolf's Charter of 1611 (**I**), and possibly also in the Form of Government of 1634 (**V**). In Gustav Adolf's time, indeed, the relations between crown and aristocracy had been fairly good, thanks to the intimate collaboration of King and Chancellor (**IV**). But during the years of Christina's minority royalists feared, or professed to fear, the eclipse of the crown by a narrow, dominant oligarchy of Council-families (**IX**). Christina roundly accused them of aiming at a kind of Polish republic; and it was in part her concern for the future of the dynasty and the authority of the crown that led her to force through the recognition of Karl Gustav as her successor, and as hereditary prince. The climax of this dynastic and constitutional question coincided with the Diet of 1650, at which the social crisis reached its first acute phase; and Christina used this coincidence to secure her objectives. After inciting the lower Estates to press their attack on the aristocracy, she struck a bargain with the first Estate: in return for her protection against the threat of a Reduction, she obtained their consent to the dynastic arrangement in Karl Gustav's favour.

The events of 1650 also marked a stage in the development of Swedish parliamentary institutions. Since 1632 the Estates had been growing in experience and confidence, and had on occasion even advanced a claim to a voice in the selection of ministers (**VI**, **IX**). In 1650 they went further. They seized the initiative for the first time (**X**); they put forward joint resolutions of three Estates; and by contending that no title could be considered good once the Estates had called it in question (**XXIV**) they advanced a claim which was truly revolutionary. They did not, however, as might have been expected, use the crown's financial straits as a lever to secure control over supply: their object was rather to make supply unnecessary by enabling the crown once more to live of its own. The lower Estates looked upon the crown as their ally against the aristocracy, and they feared the prerogative a good deal less than the pretensions of the first Estate. If their proceedings in 1650 had seemed almost revolutionary to constitutional conservatives, it was not against the crown that their revolution was directed. It was during Christina's minority, and against the Council, that the Estates had first developed their pretensions; and not until the next minority were those pretensions renewed (**XI**). And if, as then happened, there should be friction between the Regents and the Council, the Diet would tend to support the Regents (as the temporary custodians of the prerogative) rather than the Council (as permanent depositaries of constitutional principle) (**XII**).

When the century opened, Sweden had an administrative system which was still essentially the same as in Gustav Vasa's time. Monarchy was paternal and personal, the central government unorganized and rudimentary. The strains of foreign war, and the prolonged absences of the monarch, compelled a modernization and expansion of this antique machinery. The bases for it were laid in Gustav Adolf's time by Axel Oxenstierna: the results of his labours are summed up in the Form of Government (**V**). As the business of the state expanded and grew more complex, the demand for skilled civil servants increased. For the most part it was filled from the local resources, by graduates of the University of Uppsala, which Gustav Adolf had finally put on its legs again; but there was also an appreciable intake of foreign experts. By the middle of the century the old dislike of the 'rule of secretaries', though it still persisted, was powerless in the face of the obvious need for persons of this type. Sweden's career as a great power, among other effects, enforced the recruitment of a trained bureaucracy, which before the century was out would be politically formidable. Since the state took able men wherever it could find them, and promotion was mainly on merit, expansion of the bureaucracy brought with it a quickening of social mobility. It also helped to swell the numbers of the aristocracy, since a peerage came more and more to be the natural reward of the successful civil servant, whatever his social origins. On the other hand, the old nobility was itself a serving nobility, which as a matter of course sent its sons into the civil service or the armed forces: partly because these were the roads to rewards and favours, partly because the emoluments attached to them were not matters of indifference. It consequently happened that the new upstart bureaucrats and the needier scions of the old nobility found that they had one important interest in common, namely, the punctual payment of their wages (**XII**, **XIV**). But of this they could never be sure: indeed, they could be certain that every emergency in foreign policy would see their wages fall into arrear. For them too, as for the lower Estates who were burdened by the taxation which the crown was forced to impose, it was becoming a matter of importance that the King should again live of his own.

The crisis of 1650 did not pass away wholly without trace. The peasants were in 1652 given some protection against excessive labour-services. And Karl Gustav, from the moment of his accession in 1654, was determined that there should be a Reduction of some sort. The 'quarter-part Reduction' of 1655 (**XXVI**), brought moderate gains to the crown, and would have brought more had it not been for the King's continuous absence abroad: the same spirited foreign policy which had produced the need for a Reduction prevented its proper implementation. In 1655 the nobility accepted the Reduction reluctantly, as a matter of tactics, and in the hope that it might prove a final settlement. But in the sixties and seventies they began to change their attitude: it was not only that many of them were ready for a further Reduction in order to be sure of their wages, it was also that a Reduction was coming to look like the best means of salvaging their fundamental privilege of exemption from taxation. In the past three decades that privilege had been progressively undermined, by pleas of state necessity and appeals to the nobility's patriotism, until in fact the nobility now paid 'contributions' almost as regularly as other Estates paid taxes. To recover their fiscal immunity, many were now anxious for a Reduction who had formerly opposed it (**XXIX**). A Reduction would in any case fall most heavily (they imagined) on the high nobility – those great Council families whose social pretensions and pre-emption of the best jobs was already angering other members of the first Estate (**XXVII**). When to these considerations were added the disasters of the war of 1675-9, and the financial abysses which that war revealed, a large section of the nobility was ready to join with the non-noble Estates in making scapegoats of the Council and the ex-Regents, and to go to great lengths to put the crown upon a sound financial footing (**XIV**, **XV**). And if the fall of the Council should also entail the sacrifice of those constitutional doctrines of which the Council was the historic champion, few were disposed to regret the passing of a constitutional tradition which now seemed antiquated and irrelevant to the times.

In 1680, there could be no doubt of it, most men saw the only hope for the country in a strong monarchy, committed to a programme of peace, retrenchment and reform. Karl XI gave them most of what they wanted. A comprehensive Reduction was agreed to without difficulty (**XXIX**); after initial heavy taxation the finances made a great recovery, so that by the beginning of the nineties the budget was balanced, and the King could indeed live of his own (**XVI**); the army was reformed, and its maintenance arranged for on an automatic basis. For the first time for a generation Sweden was able to conduct a foreign policy unhampered by the ties of foreign subsidies; and that policy was suited to her capacities and designed to keep the country out of war (**XLIII**). The peasantry was saved from whatever had been the dangers that beset them. The bureaucracy was assured of its wages, and became (with the King at its head) the strongest force in the state. The power of the high nobility was broken; the Council of the Realm became the King's Council. And in the reaction against the impecuniousness, the muddle, and the military disasters of the seventies, the nation threw the reins on the King's back: by almost casual resolutions of successive Diets Karl XI became an absolute monarch – though his absolutism, as he would have been the first to point out, was absolutism within the law – and the Estates became little more than the loyal echo of the monarch's voice (**XVI, XVII**).

By 1697, when Karl XI died at the age of 41, the country had at last adapted itself to the stresses set up by its career as a great power. That career was indeed over: it had been over since 1660. But though there could be no going back (despite Karl XII) to the great days of Gustav Adolf and Karl X Gustav, the legacy of Sweden's imperial adventure could not be ignored or renounced. It had somehow to be lived with and made the best of; and it was Karl XI's achievement to have made a serious attempt to face this problem. It is not certain that he intended absolutism to be a permanent solution; and the event proved that constitutional traditions and parliamentary life could survive even his son's reign, and emerge in 1719 with unprecedented vigour. But after 1680 the social problem was permanently eased. And in foreign policy he produced a model for the conduct of a second-class power which neither Hats nor Caps would be able to emulate.

A

KING, COUNCIL AND DIET

The rule of Karl IX had provoked widespread discontent, even among his former political allies and tools, the Estate of Peasantry; and all classes seized the opportunity of a change of ruler to extort guarantees or concessions from the crown. Most of them were embodied in the Accession Charter of Gustav Adolf (**I**). By the Resolution of the Diet of Norrköping (1604) the King was not to be admitted to full control of the government until he reached the age of 24. In return for waiving this provision the Estates were able to impose explicit guarantees against misgovernment. The Clergy obtained a confirmation of the monopoly of Lutheranism (§§ 1–2), and assurance of ecclesiastical self-government (§7); the Nobility (who were at the same time granted an extension of their privileges) were promised a dominant place in the government of the state (§§ 3, 5), and obtained a pledge that there should be no repetition of the more odious features of Karl IX's rule (§10). The Charter represents the acceptance by the monarchy of the constitutional and administrative programme of the aristocracy, the limitation of royal authority, the guarantee of the rule of law (§§4–6, 8–10). The 'rule of secretaries' is implicitly condemned (§5); the authority of the Council of the Realm reaffirmed; and the practice of obtaining the consent of the Diet to legislation or taxation is diluted into 'the consent of those who are concerned' (§6). In appearance, it is a sharp defeat for the crown. In reality, the reconciliation of crown and aristocracy, incorporate in the persons of Gustav Adolf and Axel Oxenstierna (**IV**) took the sting out of the Charter, and made a literal observance of §6 in all its points unnecessary: this was particularly true in regard to foreign policy.

I Gustav Adolf's Accession Charter, 31 December 1611

Gustav Adolf promises

In the first place, that We will hold, maintain and protect all the Estates of the realm of Sweden, spiritual and lay, higher and lower, in the Christian religion, God's pure and plain Word, and the right and true use of the Holy Sacrament, which is grounded upon the sacred, prophetic and apostolic Scriptures and on the unaltered Confession of

Augsburg; and that We will not either by threats or inducements encourage or enjoin upon any of the Estates, higher or lower, . . . any other religion; nor will We permit to any man, of what nation, estate, or condition soever, the exercise or practice, in public or in private, of any other religion than as aforesaid, in this our kingdom and the provinces which pertain to it.

In the second place. That no person of any other religion, whether Papist, Calvinist, Anabaptist, or any other than that aforesaid, may be employed in any office of the realm, except that in the case of foreigners of another religion whose presence is desirable for economic or military reasons, permission will be given to them to remain in the country and follow their lawful callings, so long as they make no disturbance, do not disseminate their superstition, nor decry or insult our religion (for no sovereign has power to direct and rule a man's conscience). But for those who can be proved to have comported themselves otherwise, we shall see to it that they be suitably punished.

In the third place, We will maintain the written law of the land, the ancient rights, liberties and lawful customs of the realm; and We will preserve to all the Estates their due dignity, authority and reputation, so that nothing may happen which may be a mock or a dishonour to any of them, and so that each Estate severally be maintained in its established liberties, privileges, immunities and lawful customs, without cavil, infringement or interruption, and especially that the Estate of Nobles may be maintained and held in honour; and enjoy, for their life and their honour, their lands and their servants, the law of Sweden and all their established liberties and privileges.

In the fourth place, We promise and declare that We will rule and govern our realm of Sweden according to the royal oath as contained in the Land Law.

In the fifth place, We will cause appointments to be made to the high offices of the realm; which are: the Steward, the Marshal, the Admiral, the Chancellor, the Treasurer; as also to others of the Council and the Exchequer Council, and to the office of judge and governor in each province, and to the command in the main fortresses of the kingdom, of inborn men of the Nobility; and to the office of county court judge likewise of Swedish men, and especially of the Nobility who may be serviceable thereto, with the lawful consent of those whom it concerns, according to the law of Sweden. And it is likewise our will to provide, for those who by Us are employed in the highest offices of the realm, a necessary maintenance from the fiefs and revenues of the crown, which will vary according to the service, office and condition of each of them, in conformity with the ordinance which We purpose to make thereupon, with the advice of our Council. Nor will We degrade or remove any from such office, without he be lawfully sentenced to lose it in a court of law.

In the sixth place, We will make no new law, nor impose any upon the Estates, nor will we alter, suppress or rescind any old and accepted law, without the approval, consent and participation of the highborn Prince, Duke Johan, the Council of the Realm, and all the Estates, as the law and our royal oath require. Nor will We suffer any injunction or prohibition to issue, nor make any ordinance concerning the kingdom in general without the knowledge and advice of the Council of the Realm, and the consent of those who are concerned. Much less shall any royal officer, higher or lower, have power to impose upon the commonalty any aid or tax, great or small, without our order and assent. And when an ordinance is thus lawfully made, or an injunction or prohibition is issued, We will not alter or revoke it, nor grant to any man a particular dispensation from it; without prejudice, however, to existing privileges. Nor will We burden the Estates with many Diets, unless there be special need for it, and the reasons for their summons have previously been considered and approved by the Council of the Realm; nor will We begin or embark upon any war or campaign, nor enter into or conclude any peace, truce or alliance with any potentate or republic, without the knowledge and consent of the highborn Duke Johan, the Council of the Realm, and the Estates.

In the seventh place, We have also promised that the election of bishops be held according to the Church Ordinance now in force and agreed to, and that they be permitted their due and lawful power and authority to ordain priests, and to present them to livings (with the consent of the congregation, and saving the rights of patrons) according to the tenour and content of the Church Ordinance aforesaid, so that hereafter no priest need seek confirmation of Us, except for those livings of special importance, commonly called royal benefices, which henceforward are to be specified in the revised Church Ordinance which We shall cause to be printed. Nor will We permit that any of the clergy be refused his living and office, much less deprived, without previous investigation before the Chapter; nor (in the event of his being found culpable) that he be degraded and deprived by any other than the bishop in whose diocese he is, and in the manner laid down in the printed Swedish Church Ordinance which appeared in the year

[15]72. . . . We will also maintain the Academy at Uppsala, providing it with such privileges, and granting to bishops, professors, urban pastors and schoolmasters such a maintenance, as We with our well-beloved Council of the Realm may judge necessary to them and feasible in the present state of the kingdom.

In the eighth place: In order that no man may have cause to complain of law, justice, or its execution, We will appoint, in those places which are still inadequately provided with judges, bailiffs, constables and clerks, such native Swedish men as may be able and serviceable thereto, that they may protect our subjects (as well poor as rich) from violence and wrong, and help them to their law and right. Nor will We suffer that any foreigner be appointed to any office in any town, either to be burgomaster, councillor, town-clerk, clerk of the customs . . . or any other office, according to the ordinance and statute made in Stockholm by the Council of the Realm in the year 1470.

In the ninth place: We will not suffer that any provincial judge hold county court in his own province, nor that any bailiff be county court judge in his own bailiwick; nor will We permit that the sums designed for the payment of such judges be applied to any other purpose than to the maintenance of those who are to dispense the law. It is likewise our will that even as every man freely may hold and enjoy his lawful possessions until he is deprived of them by lawful doom, so none shall presume to appropriate to himself any property which has been refused him, or of which he has been deprived, by lawful sentence of a court.

And lastly: In order that none may suffer any wrong, but every man have the benefit of his innocency and his good cause, therefore have We promised and declared that should any charge, of whatever nature, be brought to Us against any man (as may happen, from jealousy or false report), We will not cause him forthwith to be imprisoned or arrested, nor allow him to be slighted in his honour or good name, nor will We take away or give away or in any way deprive him of his land or property, before and unless he is convicted and sentenced for the same; but that in future he shall be proceeded against by trial and judgment, as the law of the land lays down and requires. And if any man delate or traduce another, We will disclose his identity, so that he may answer at law to him whom he has accused. . . .

At Nyköping, the last day of December, in the year 1611.

Svenska riksdagsakter, I Series, II, i, 70-6

II The *riksdag*-Ordinance of 1617

The immediate circumstances which provoked this Ordinance are set out in **II**(*a*). It was never formally subscribed by the Estates, and so was never promulgated as a statute; but its procedures did in fact form the basis for the future rules of order of the Diet, and it has an important place in the development of that body. It fixed, for instance, the number of Estates at four (the Estate of Princes soon became extinct; that of the army officers effectively merged with the Nobility). The attempt to get away from formal written procedures, and permit impromptu debate between King and Estates, was successfully resisted by Burghers and Peasants; but the personal confrontation it envisaged was exploited by Gustav Adolf, as well as by his successors, for purposes of persuasion and propaganda (**III**). The fact that the Ordinance left the King liberty to choose which opinion he thought best, in the event of discrepant answers from the Estates, had less constitutional significance than might appear: the King was still bound to rule according to law, Charter and coronation oath; and no new burden could be laid on any Estate without its assent.

(*a*)

From a parliamentary diary kept by the Queen-Mother's chancery

In the year 1617, on 24 January, His Majesty caused the Estates to be called together in the Hall of State, and there the Chancellor, Herr Axel Oxenstierna, spoke to them of the disorder and confusion which is wont to prevail at meetings of the Estates here in Sweden, which he said had been, and still was, a matter of much concern to His Majesty whenever he thought of it. . . . As to the disorder which has prevailed at former meetings of the Diet, and which prevails still, [he mentioned, as an example of it] how members of the one Estate run in and out among members of the others in places where business is to be done, so that the Estates have become so intermingled that it has been impossible to tell the one from the other, but here stands a nobleman, there a priest, here a burgher and there a peasant, all mixed up together, and in such disorder that persons who ought to have been at the far end of the room have the foremost seats, and those who ought to take the first place must be content with the last. As a result of this state of affairs, many spies and agents who have not the slightest interest in the matters which are to be dealt with at the Diet have insinuated themselves into the meetings, whose object is not so much the discussion of what may be for the nation's good, but rather espionage, very much to its detriment. And this sort of disorder and confusion is not only prejudicial to us . . . but it is also contemptible and humiliating abroad, where they laugh at it and deride it. And it is deplorable that at meetings such as these, where matters of such high importance to the realm are to be dealt with, with implications for His Majesty, the Estates and the whole country, we cannot proceed in a more orderly fashion. Even at a county court or a parish meeting, after all, the judge has his appointed place, the jury has theirs, and when a decision or a judgment is to be pronounced each moves to his appropriate position. But at a Diet, where matters of such importance are to be transacted, all sorts are jumbled together from beginning to end. In this matter the Estate of Clergy is clear of blame, and the Burghers nearly so; but in the Nobility (of which Estate he counts himself a member, and so may the more candidly tell them his opinion and their faults) there is much that is amiss; as for instance that many of them, when matters of the greatest consequence are under discussion, hold dinner-parties, or themselves go to dinner with someone else, and thereby waste time, and fail to take the business seriously, but rather hold it of small account. And the Commonalty, when the points in the King's Proposition are communicated to them, tend to run around for scriveners, and maybe (as has happened in the past) hit upon a bunch of spies and intriguers to write their answer for them, so that before a fair copy of it has reached the King a copy of the Proposition is in the hands of the enemy: this happened in the case of two rogues, . . . who on previous occasions hung about the Diet and got themselves employed to write the answers of the Commonalty, and then made off to Poland with the original of the Proposition, and revealed everything that was done at the Diet. For this reason, in order to prevent this kind of thing for the future, His Majesty has caused an ordinance to be drafted, including both rules of procedure and directions as to how the Proposition is to be debated, and the answer to it communicated.

Svenska riksdagsakter, I Series, II, ii, 23-4

(*b*)

The King's Proposition concerning an Ordinance for the Diet. Örebro, 24 January 1617

First. When the Diet is to begin, then the Estates shall assemble in the Hall of State, and there a place is appointed for the King, the Hereditary Princes, the Council of the Realm, and for each Estate severally, as also for every member of each Estate, as follows [the placing described].

As soon as His Majesty has greeted the Estates and opened the Diet, the points of the King's Proposition shall be handed over to the Estates to consider;

Thereupon . . . the Estates shall separate, each to its own chamber, to consider the points, and to draw up its answer and observations upon them in writing. . . . His Majesty will then come in to them, and each Estate severally will deliver its answer in writing, through its representative, to His Majesty, and thereafter explain the reasons which have led them to make it. . . .

If the King is satisfied with the answer, well and good; if there is matter of difficulty in it, His Majesty replies either orally or in writing, as the importance of the point may require. If there is any discrepancy between the resolutions of the Estates, then each Estate may defend and maintain its opinion through one of its members, in the presence of His Majesty, so that after the reasons and arguments have been heard, they can be weighed one against the other, and a conclusion reached as to which is most firmly based, until in the end the divergences are reconciled, or His Majesty takes that which appears best. . . .

And in order that all things may be done with the more order and secrecy, His Majesty will provide the Commonalty with sworn clerks, to take their votes and draw up their answers.

Ibid., 84-7

III King and Estates: Gustav Adolf's farewell speech to the Estates, 19 May 1630

This famous speech is a good example of the King's style of oratory (for another, see **XXXI**), and of his ability to use the opportunities afforded by parliamentary institutions to associate his people with his policies, and with himself. Most of the major decisions of the reign were carefully prepared and buttressed by the support of the Diet: he believed in spreading the responsibility, wherever possible. The personal tie between sovereign and subjects which was created by these means was an important element of strength to the state. The terms of the farewell to the Clergy are notable: the slightly tart flavour of his exhortation to them is no doubt to be attributed to the resistance of the episcopate to his schemes for remodelling church-government.

. . . Thereupon they [the Nobility] went up to the Hall of State, where the other Estates were already assembled.

Then His Majesty entered, in converse with the Council of the

Realm, and after he had sat down, Dr Salvius read out the Resolution, as it stood written on the parchment.

Thereupon H.M. graciously thanked them all, for that like loyal subjects they had consented to and granted what at this time was requisite to the safety of the state; and conjured them dutifully and cheerfully to make their promise good.

Then H.M. said: that he could well imagine the hardships which conscription entailed; yet if they would but consider it a little more closely it had great advantages too, since they had now these many years (thank God) been able with Swedish men to carry the war into the enemy's country, and so shift the burden of it to their foes; so that H.M., under the protection and providence of God, had by Swedish soldiers taken and subjected great towns and provinces, and now with diplomatic help from the Kings of France and England, and the Elector of Brandenburg, had so far constrained the enemy that he had brought himself to agree to a truce of six years [the Truce of Altmark, 1629]. And since H.M. was now got into a war with the Emperor and his adherents, more onerous and of greater scope than the former, he hoped they would, as faithful subjects, accept the conscription cheerfully, or else give an aid instead of it . . . and that, as in the past, they would loyally do their share to support H.M. in this new conflict.

Thereafter H.M. took his farewell of each of the Estates.

'And since it is wont to fall out that the pitcher is borne so often to the well that it is broken at last, so will it be with me; that I, who now in so many dangers and occasions have shed my blood for the welfare of the Swedish realm – though hitherto by the gracious protection of God without forfeit of my life – must lose it also at the last: therefore on this last occasion before my departure I would commend you all, the subjects and Estates of this realm, present and absent, to the care of Almighty God, in soul, body and estate, in the hope that after this evil and painful life we may by God's pleasure meet once more in that heavenly and eternal life and gladness which is prepared by God for us. In particular I commend to the all-powerful God you of the Council of the Realm, wishing you with all my heart that you may never lack for good counsel, and that you may so perform your office that God's honour and His holy Word and doctrine may be kept pure among us, and be preserved in our fatherland to our posterity; and next, that peace and unity may grow and flourish among you, and all ill-will, disunion and strife may be avoided and done away, and that good counsel never fail you, to the safety, security and repose of the fatherland; and finally that you may never lack for successors, but that there may grow up such a new generation as may bring strength, assistance, and upright dealing to the service of government and country. And this I wish you with all my heart, by way of valediction.

'In like measure I commend you of the Nobility to the safekeeping of the Almighty God, desiring that you may so continue in manliness and knightly qualities that you and your posterity may once more cause the far-flung fame and immortal name of your Gothic ancestors – now long forgotten, yea, almost held in contempt by other nations – to be known over the whole world, so that it may shine again with fresh lustre; as it will do, if those who during my reign have borne themselves so nobly, and so gallantly spared neither blood nor life, continue in that resolution, whereby you have shewn yourselves to be the true heirs and descendants of the ancient Goths, who in their day conquered almost the whole earth, and brought many kingdoms into subjection, and so ruled for hundreds of years: I wish, then, that you may once more suffer yourselves to be led out to war; whereby, having gained an immortal fame, the respect of Kings and Princes, and broad acres as your reward, you will with the better reputation discharge the duties of your noble Estate. All this we now desire for you, in this our valediction.

'Of you of the spiritual Estate I take my leave also, exhorting you to adjure your congregations, whose hearts are in your power to twist and turn as you will, to be faithful and true to their governors, and to do their duty cheerfully and obediently, confirming them in all unity and concord, so that they be not led astray by evil men. And you shall not only exhort and persuade them thereto, but shall also yourselves show them the way, by your decent and modest bearing; so that they keep themselves quiet and conformable not only by reason of your learned sermons, but by the example of your behaviour. Above all be on your guard that you do not, by the sin of pride, provoke resentment against you. Seek diligently to attain to righteousness; have a care of factions; and at all times so admonish your flocks (whose heart is in your hands, to persuade to good or to evil) that they comport themselves tractably and quietly, giving to the crown and to their landlords whatever may be their due. And this I wish for you with all my heart.

'For you of the burghers, I wish that your little cabins may become great mansions, your small boats great ships and merchantmen, and that the oil in your cruse fail not. And this is my valediction to you.

'For the Commonalty and Peasantry, it is my wish that their meadows may be green, their fields bear an hundredfold, so that their barns may be full; and that they may increase and multiply in all plenteousness, that with gladness and without sighing they may be able to discharge the duties and obligations that lie upon them.

'And in sum I do commend you, all and several, in soul and body, to the Almighty God.'

C. G. Styffe, *Konung Gustaf II Adolfs Skrifter*, pp. 628–33

IV King and minister

The collaboration of Gustav Adolf and Axel Oxenstierna was based not only upon the close approximation of their views on politics, but on a growing reciprocal trust, which in the end ripened to real affection. This is not the only letter in which that feeling appears, but it is certainly the most remarkable. The King discloses, with complete frankness, his anxiety at the prospect of what may happen after his death. He had no illusions about the unfitness of his neurotic wife for the office of Regent, and it was in accordance with his known views that she was excluded, after his death, from all share in the government.

Gustav Adolf to Axel Oxenstierna: Gollnow, 4 December 1630

Trusty and well-beloved, I greet you well.

I have received your advice regarding next year's campaign: it says much for your fidelity to me and to the fatherland. Assuming that we survive, your plans seem to have a good chance of success, and you may expect to gain the applause of posterity – particularly if you reinforce good counsel with your habitual zeal and energy in executing it. I wish there were others who could deal with our affairs with the same discretion, fidelity, and knowledge: if there were, I am sure that the country's service and the welfare of us all would be safer than it is at present. But as God bestows His gifts upon us, so also our sins ensure that we shall all have faults of one sort or another; and I confess that I find them so great in some of those who are concerned in the affairs of state that I am often near to losing hope of any good outcome, if God did not now and then give heavenly counsel when no other counsel was to be had. Do your best, then; do not weary of the service of King and country; for I would rather trust my welfare to your zeal than to any other man's. May God the Protector of us all help us to get through this winter; for I count on things becoming easier next summer, thanks to your energy and care. So far, God has vouchsafed us a measure of hard-won success: may He now grant us grace that our righteous cause may triumph and come to a good end, to the honour of His most holy name, the peace and quietness of His church, and the salvation of us all in this world and the next! I would have sent you a description of our present situation, but the bullets I stopped at Dirschau have made my hand stiff, so that I cannot do it. But I may tell you that the enemy is weak in infantry, a match for us in cavalry, and has great advantage in the matter of quarters, for the whole of Germany is his to plunder. I am gathering my troops together here on the river, and intend shortly to attack him and try to push him out of his quarters; but though I have a good and righteous cause, the fortunes of war are as uncertain for us poor sinners as the life of man. And so I urge and entreat you, for Christ's sake, not to lose heart if the issue be otherwise than we would have it. I know that I may rely upon you to take care of my memory, and to look after the welfare of my family as you would that God should look after you and yours – and as I myself will look after them, if God permits me to live so long that you should need my help in that way. For nearly twenty years I have fought my country's battle; with no small difficulty, it is true, but also (thank God) with some credit; I have loved and honoured our fatherland and all loyal subjects that dwell in it, and for its sake have ventured life and estate and lived laborious days; and I have sought no other reward in this life than to do my duty in the state to which God hath called me. If anything should happen to me, my family will become objects of compassion; for they are women, the mother a person of no judgment, the daughter still a young girl; likely to make a mess of things if they are given their head; in danger, if others gain an ascendancy over them. Natural affection forces these lines from my pen in order to prepare you – as an instrument sent to me from God to light me through many a dark place – for what may happen: it is, in all the world, the care which weighs heaviest upon me. Yet this too, as also my life and soul and everything that God has given me, I commend into His keeping; hoping always the best in this world, and after this life peace, and joy, and felicity. And the same I wish for you when your hour shall come.

I remain, for as long as I live, ever your gracious and affectionate

Gustav Adolf

Axel Oxenstiernas skrifter och brevvexling, II, i, 669-70

V The Form of Government, 1634

Eight days after the battle of Lützen, Axel Oxenstierna sent over to Sweden a draft of the document printed below. Earlier drafts had been in existence since the mid-twenties; and one of them is known to have been discussed between Oxenstierna and Gustav Adolf at Nuremberg in 1632. It was important for the Council of the Realm to be able to adduce the argument that the project had the dead King's sanction: hence the careful wording of the preamble and the closing paragraph. Not all contemporaries believed it: Queen Christina later professed to doubt whether her father had ever read a word of it. And it has been contended that it was in effect a programme for oligarchical rule, foisted on the nation under cover of the King's name; a consolidation of the victory won by the aristocracy over the monarchy in 1611 (**I**); a step, perhaps, towards something like the Polish type of crowned republic: the words 'for ever', at the close of the preamble (importing a fundamental law) were thought to point in this direction, and were accepted by the Diet only after a difficult passage. Oxenstierna's political rivals and enemies (and at least one modern historian) suspected the Chancellor of concocting the document as a springboard for his family ambitions. The Form of Government does indeed represent the realization of a long-standing aristocratic demand for better government and more modern administrative methods; and its success in this respect is confirmed by the high reputation it enjoyed abroad. But it is also the codification and completion of the work of administrative reform which had been one of the great initiatives of Gustav Adolf's reign (see §§ 5-43). And it provided also, in §§ 53-64, some urgently needed, automatically-functioning machinery for the carrying on of the government in the case of the sovereign's incapacity or absence (e.g. on foreign campaigns). Both these objects must certainly have been as important to Gustav Adolf as to Oxenstierna. No doubt the Form of Government *could* have been used as a stalking-horse for the interests of a narrow aristocratic class, consolidating its political power at the expense of the monarchy; but it does not seem in fact that the Regents attempted anything of the sort. On the contrary, they took great care to safeguard the prerogative (see §§ 56-7, 59-64). It seems likely, on the whole, that it does represent something near to Gustav Adolf's intentions; and this may well be true even of those clauses (§§ 43-5, 58) which constitute a potential danger to the development of true parliamentary institutions: Gustav Adolf rather fell out of love with Diets in his closing years. He might have objected to 'for ever'; but the course of events in fact proved that the Form of Government, so far from being eternal, could not survive a minority.

[After a lengthy preamble emphasizing that Gustav Adolf had drafted the Form of Government in his lifetime, as a precaution against civil strife, and in order to ensure the establishment of 'a regular government, in which the King's Majesty, the Council's authority, and the reasonable rights and liberties of the

Estates were secured to each and in some degree defined', there follows the Form of Government as Gustav Adolf was alleged to have drawn it: this begins with a second preamble, which concludes:]

We have accordingly discussed this matter with our well-beloved Council, and afterwards with those Estates whom it concerns, and have after ripe consideration, and with their advice and consent, caused to be drawn up an ordinance and statute, which is to be held and observed for ever, as follows:

1

Since unity in religion . . . is the unshakable foundation of a sound, united and enduring government, it is enacted that henceforward Kings, office-holders and subjects shall adhere to the pure and plain Word of God, as it stands in the prophetic and apostolic Scriptures; as it is expounded in the creeds, Luther's catechism, and the unaltered Confession of Augsburg; and as it is established by the decisions of the Council of Uppsala [1593] and the resolutions of the Diet and the charters of the realm.

2

The succession to the throne shall be according to the Succession Pact made in Västerås in the year 1544, renewed and amplified at Norrköping in the year 1604, and now last applied and modified in favour of our beloved daughter Christina at Stockholm in the year 1627.

3

It is the King's right to rule and govern his lands and castles, and all that pertains to him and the crown, as the law lays down.

4

Since the land is of great extent, and its concerns so many and weighty that the King cannot handle them alone, he stands in need of counsellors, officers and captains to aid him, and these he chooses according to the law of Sweden, the needs of the realm, and his own good pleasure.

5

It has of old time been, and shall hereafter be, that next to the King's Majesty the highest dignity in the realm shall pertain to the Council of the Realm, whom the King is to choose from native-born knights and esquires; and although their number neither has been nor can be fixed (since as many are like to be appointed as the necessities and honour of the country require) yet it shall ordinarily be 25, including the five great officers of state. . . . It shall be their common and particular concern to put the King in mind of the law of the land; to advise him to the best of their ability as may be most advantageous for him and the realm; to strengthen the Estates and the commonalty in fidelity and compliance; and in all other matters that may come before them, ordinary or extraordinary, to have a constant care for the rights, dignity, advantage and welfare of King and people, according to the oath which they have sworn to each.

6

. . . All matters which concern or arise from the government shall ordinarily be distributed among, and dealt with by, one of the following five Colleges or fraternities, according to the nature of the business: namely, the Supreme Court, the War Council, the Admiralty, the Chancery, the Exchequer; saving always the King's rights and prerogatives.

7

[Functions of the Supreme Court described]

8

[The Supreme Court divided into four branches, all of equal authority] The first, and the senior in dignity, is the Supreme Court in Stockholm, where the Steward is to preside; and shall consist (besides him) of 16 persons or assessors, whereof four are to be of the Council of the Realm, six of the Nobility, and six of other learned and able men. . . .

These Supreme Courts, each in its district, shall consider and decide all cases which properly come before them, and from their judgment there shall be no appeal; saving that any man who feels himself in any way aggrieved is entitled to present a complaint to the King, and petition him for a revision of the judgment.

9

If any misdemean himself who is of such high estate, or employed in so great an office, that it touches the King's Majesty, and the case cannot therefore conveniently be investigated and decided save by the Estates of the Realm, then all the members of all the Supreme Courts shall be summoned (by us or our successors) and they, together with the rest of the Council, those provincial governors who may be available, and one burgomaster each from Stockholm, Uppsala, Göteborg, Norrköping, Åbo, and Viborg, shall act for the Estates and have power to pronounce judgment on the case; and no one, however exalted his condition, shall have leave to decline their jurisdiction; and in such cases the Steward shall always preside. . . .

10

The second College is the War Council, which is to be directed by the Marshal, who shall have as assessors two of the Council of the Realm (and especially those who are or have been serving officers) and four other officers, either now or formerly on active service. . . .

[Its functions defined; control of finance to be reserved to the Exchequer]

11

The third College is the Admiralty, where the Admiral of the Realm presides, having as assessors two of the Council of the Realm, preferably such as have seen sea service, and four vice-admirals, or the senior and most capable captains, whereof the port-admiral or -captain is always to be one.

[Its functions defined; control of finance to be reserved to the Exchequer]

12

The fourth College is the Chancery, over which the Chancellor presides, having as assessors four of the Council of the Realm . . . and two secretaries of state, preferably of the Nobility.

[Duties of the Chancery described]

The ordinary meetings of the Council of the Realm shall be arranged by the Chancellor, and shall be held in the innermost chamber of the Chancery. . . .

. . . All state documents, before they are submitted to the King for his signature, shall be scrutinized and signed by the Chancellor or his deputy. . . .

13

The fifth and last College is the Exchequer, in which the Treasurer presides, and has as assessors two of the Council of the Realm, two of the Nobility, and two of the most senior Exchequer-Councillors.

14

These five Colleges (except, of course, the provincial Supreme Courts) shall ordinarily sit in Stockholm . . . [the precise location of each being prescribed]. . . . And all of them shall remain constantly at the King's court in Stockholm, year in and year out, so that irrespective of whether one or other of the persons appointed to them may be absent (whether on other service, or on leave) the College shall notwithstanding continue to function, and be constantly at work. Except that it may from time to time be refreshed and solaced with some vacations and holidays.

. . . .

16

[Individual members of the Colleges have no authority as such save when functioning *as* members *in* the College, whose authority and powers are strictly corporate.]

17

[No College to poach on another's territory, nor meddle in another's business.]

. . . .

23

The local administration of the country is to be divided into provinces or governments after the following manner: the first is that of the lord-lieutenant of Stockholm, always to be a member of the Council of the Realm, having his residence in Stockholm Castle; the second, the governor of Uppland. . . . [A list of a further 21 provinces follows, including Finland and the Baltic provinces.]

. . . .

26

[Fourteen judicial divisions, each with its provincial judge, to hear appeals from county courts.]

27

No man may be governor in the government wherein he is provincial judge; no governor shall have charge of any castle or fortress intended for defence, still less have power to appoint or remove the commander of such a place, or exercise any authority over the crown's castles, fortresses or fortifications....

. . . .

30

Governorships, as well as the command of castles, shall ordinarily be for a term of three years, after which time ... the holders shall be replaced by others, and they shall present themselves in Stockholm and there before all the five Colleges give an account of their administration, each matter being referred to the appropriate College, and so bear witness to their fidelity to the King's service.... If they be found to have been unfaithful or neglectful, they are to be prosecuted by the Public Prosecutor before the Supreme Court, and suffer the penalties prescribed by the law. [The King has power to prolong terms of office at need.]

31

There shall be 28 regiments – 8 of horse, 20 of foot – each of a size proportionate to its province. [A list follows.]

33-4

[Provisions to ensure that civil and military authorities do not meddle in each other's sphere.]

36

Every office-holder shall be bound to give on the appointed day an account of his administration, either to the King himself if he has time for it, or in ordinary circumstances as follows: all judges or judicial officers – to the Supreme Court; all military officers – to the War Council; all those concerned with the navy, or with the building or furnishing of ships of war – to the Admiralty; provincial governors, ambassadors, and agents – to the Chancery, in so far as their business concerns it; and lastly all officials who have to do, directly or indirectly, with the revenue or expenditure of the kingdom ... to the Exchequer; and there render their report for the preceding year.

. . . .

38

. . . The aforementioned five Colleges shall, every year, from Epiphany to Candlemas, revise, examine, investigate and scrutinize the papers, transactions and acts of all others who are employed about the court or in local government, and correct anything that may emerge in the light of the instruction issued by the College in question. And in like manner they shall themselves, from Candlemas to Ash Wednesday, each make their own report to the King in person . . . or in his absence to the five great officers of state, the lord-lieutenant of Stockholm acting as deputy for the occasion in place of whichever of the great officers is presenting his College's report. First shall be taken the report of the Steward and his College, whose minutes, acts, judgments and resolutions shall be produced and scrutinized; next, from the Marshal . . . [etc.].

[In an emergency, the examination may be done by experienced deputies.]

39

On 1 June, or at the latest at Michaelmas, the presidents in the other three Supreme Courts [i.e. Jönköping, Åbo, Dorpat], or the vice-presidents, with two assessors and the clerk of the court, shall present themselves in Stockholm, and likewise give an account and report (either to the King or to the aforesaid five great officers) of their proceedings, and subject to the same penalties as the others.

41

[Procedure for trial of members of Colleges, or of whole Colleges, accused of criminal conduct.]

. . . .

43

At this annual meeting of the officers of the realm, care shall be taken to collect the best information about everything relating to the condition of the country and the circumstances of the people; and the opportunity may be taken, after consultation with them, to deal with such matters as do not require a general Diet.

44

It may happen from time to time that the opinion of the Estates is required, or that there is a matter of importance to communicate, but that it would be inexpedient to wait for the assembling of a general Diet, either because time is short, or for some other reason. In such a case it shall be referred to the aforesaid meeting of officials, afforced by two members of the Nobility from each province, the bishops and superintendents from Sweden and Finland, and one representative each from Stockholm, Uppsala, Göteborg, Norrköping, Åbo, and Viborg.

45

But when the business demands a general meeting of the Diet – as for a coronation, or other notable cause – all members of the Council of the Realm shall be present without fail, except only in the case of sickness, official duties, or absence abroad with the King's knowledge and consent. There shall also be summoned, and be bound to appear, all counts, barons, knights and esquires . . . who are come to full age, are domiciled in Sweden or Finland, and are not furnished with a lawful excuse; next, the bishops and superintendents in Sweden and Finland with two members from every chapter, and one priest from every two counties [*härader*]; further, the colonels, lieutenant-colonels, majors and one captain (of horse or foot) from every regiment, not having a lawful excuse; also one burgomaster and one town-councillor (or other leading burgher) from each town; and lastly one peasant from every county in Sweden and Finland. And these assemblies and meetings shall be accounted lawful Diets, and their resolutions be held as binding; and as not to be questioned by any loyal subject.

. . . .

48

For every office in the kingdom there shall be appointed a reasonable maintenance, suitable to the dignity and requirements of the office, and such as the budget may be able to bear; and he who is called to such an office shall be content therewith. Nor shall he without good cause withdraw himself from the service of King and country, but rather be found zealous therein, as the law requires, and as every man's oath, duty and loyalty demand.

. . . .

53

If the King, for one reason or another, is absent in foreign countries;

or if he becomes incapable through illness; or if he dies leaving a minor or an unmarried daughter to succeed him; then the five great officers of the realm (or their deputies, when they are away from Stockholm) shall corporately stand in the King's place if he be absent or ill, and after his death act as guardians and regents for his successor, if a minor or an unmarried daughter; and their bidding or forbidding shall be esteemed as the King's orders, for so long as the King is ill or absent, or the minority continues, or the princess remains unmarried.

56

In the King's absence the government shall refer all important matters to him in writing, and if possible await his decision before issuing orders or prohibitions; but if danger threatens, and would be increased by delay, they are to take such action as they may be able to justify, and as the needs of King and country require. Should the King be sick, they are to use a like discretion. . . . Should an official die, or be found negligent or incapable . . . if the office is such that it can without inconvenience be allowed to remain vacant and be discharged *ad interim* by someone else until the King has been informed and his pleasure taken thereon, then it shall be allowed to remain vacant; if not, a successor may be appointed, until the King has recovered . . . or returned home, when it will be open to him either to approve the choice or to set another in his place.

57

No new law or statute shall be made during the King's absence or illness, but the country shall be ruled according to existing law, statute and custom; no new privileges shall be issued, nor old ones confirmed . . .; no liberties, immunities or exemptions shall be granted or given to any Estate or private person; all complaints of the commonalty which are usually brought to the King shall be considered by the Regents, who shall either refer them to the appropriate College, or deal with them themselves, according to the nature of the case; and if the King be at a great distance, or his illness be desperate, they shall likewise revise and adjudicate upon cases transferred to the King, by petition of right, from the Supreme Courts, though they are bound to justify and report their action to the King upon his return or recovery. . . .

58

While the sovereign is a minor or an unmarried woman, the five great officers will carry on every part of the government on the King's behalf, save that they shall have no power to do anything which is against the law, or to the prejudice of the Succession Pact or the King's Majesty, nor to accord any privileges which tend to his disadvantage or the permanent diminution of his revenues; and in the event of their doing so the sovereign has the right to revoke what they have done, when he or she comes of age.

. . . .

60

No person shall be ennobled or naturalized as a noble while the King is abroad, or ill, or a minor; and no crown land, no freehold land nor any other of the crown's rights and sovereignties, shall be either sold, exchanged, donated, or in any other way alienated by the government; and a King may, upon his return home, or his recovery, or his majority, revoke and resume at pleasure any such alienations. . . .

61

Now it may well be that in the King's absence or illness the needs of the realm may require an alteration in law and statute, new orders or prohibitions [etc.]: such alterations shall have the force of law for as long as the King is abroad or ill; but so soon as he returns home, or recovers his health, all are referred to his consideration, and he has the right either to ratify or to revoke them. . . .

62

. . . When a minority comes to an end, and the King enters upon the government, all statutes, orders and prohibitions made during his nonage are referred to his consideration, and he has the right to ratify or revoke them, as also to confirm or remove all holders of offices, and to reaffirm or cancel resolutions; . . . provided only that matters that have been resolved at a general Diet of the Estates are to be ratified or revoked only at another meeting of the same kind. . . .

63

The government shall make no treaty or agreement with neighbouring or other foreign monarchs, republics or towns while the King is abroad or ill, unless the King has given them a general or special commission in his absence, or unless his illness seems to be incurable. . . . Nor shall they in the King's absence enter into any alliance without his special commission; and if he be incurably ill they shall do so only subject to his ratification, if he recovers, and to his successor's, if he should die.

64

But if the sovereign be a minor or an unmarried woman, the government is empowered (with the advice and assent of those who by law and statute are concerned) to determine upon and conclude peace or alliance . . . on behalf of King and kingdom; though the King is entitled to ratify and confirm it himself when he comes to his majority.

65

And if by the usual mutability of all human affairs it should happen (which God forbid) that on the death of the King there is no child or collateral heir who is entitled by the aforesaid Succession Pacts to inherit the throne, and no successor has in the meantime been designated, then the aforesaid five great officers shall carry on the government with the advice of the Council of the Realm, and according to the forms already set out, until such time as the entire Council and Estates shall have agreed upon a King.

. . . .

This Form of Government, drawn in the name of His late Majesty . . . and now rehearsed to us . . . we have diligently perused; we have duly weighed all parts of it, well considered and deliberated upon it; and now of set purpose and of our unconstrained free will we have endorsed it, approved it, enacted it, resolved it, given it the force of law, and promulgated it, as we herewith and by virtue of these presents now do in the most emphatic manner; and it is our will that it shall hereafter be obeyed and held as a law and statute by all . . . who dwell within Her Majesty's . . . dominions; and we will and require that the present government and Regency in all things conform to it and take it for a rule, and that no man presume to infringe it, on pain of Her Majesty's heavy wrath and displeasure. . . . Done in Stockholm the 29 July, in the one thousand six hundred and thirty-fourth year after the birth of Christ.

Emil Hildebrand: *Sveriges regeringsformer 1634-1809 samt konungaförsäkringar 1611-1800*, pp. 1-41

VI The Regents and the Estates, 1633-42

The period from 1632 to 1660 saw a marked growth in the political self-consciousness of the Diet. It was not a smooth progression: the claims of the Estates to be consulted, to a monopoly of legislation and taxation, to some sort of control over the executive, and finally to the initiative, came sporadically, provoked by the crises of 1634, 1650 and 1660. Some of them, e.g. the claim to sovereign authority and to jurisdiction over peccant ministers (extract (*a*)), or the principle of redress before supply (extracts (*b*) and (*c*)), or Rudbeckius' bold assertion of the legislative sovereignty of the Diet (extract (*d*)), were innovations, shocking to conservative statesmen. The Regents at first were conciliatory. But with the return of Oxenstierna from Germany in 1636 the government was given a firmness of direction which it had recently lacked: see Oxenstierna's comments on the fumblings of his colleagues in extract (*f*). The Regents were by no means certain how far they were bound to consult the Estates on such matters as raising troops, or major decisions on foreign policy; the Form of Government, after all, had left open the possibility of dealing with small committee-meetings. Oxenstierna seems at first to have inclined to prefer them, either as a matter of convenience, or because he really felt that the Estates were threatening to encroach on the sphere of the executive. After about 1638, however, he changed his mind: he enjoyed a resounding parliamentary triumph at the Diet of 1642 (**VIII**), and by the time the regency ended the danger that the full meetings of the Estates might gradually fade out in favour of more businesslike committee-meetings had passed: see Oxenstierna's explicit acknowledgment of the Diet's monopoly of taxation, in extract (*g*).

A

The claims of the Estates

(*a*)

The debates on the Form of Government in 1634 produced some startling claims. Among them the following, none of which were accepted by the government:

[The Nobility, debating §5, and in particular the words 'from native-born knights and esquires' (above, p. 19):]

Resolved: . . . That when the great officers of state are chosen and appointed, it be done with the agreement and consent of the Estates of the Realm.

Sveriges ridderskaps och adels riksdagsprotokoll, ii, 72

[On §41, the Nobility resolved:]

That since at present we have no [adult] King (which God amend), sovereignty inheres in the Estates; and therefore should a whole College, or one of the five great officers of State, be guilty of any delinquency, they are to answer and be responsible to the Estates of the Realm.

Ibid., 74

[And on §64]

That for the words 'those who . . . are concerned', may be substituted, 'with the knowledge of the Estates'.

Ibid., 130

(*b*)

1 March 1633. There entered [into the meeting of the Council] Master Petrus Bjugg, with some other members of the Clergy, with the intimation that they could make no answer [to the Proposition] until they were informed what the Council proposed to do about their grievances.

The Commander-in-Chief [Jakob de la Gardie]: We have been working on them, and you can imagine it takes time. You have had the Proposition in your hands for a fortnight, and now you demand an immediate answer to your memorandum! In any case, we had supposed that you would refrain from putting forward grievances. . . . Otherwise we really do not see how government is to be carried on if you intend to evade your obligations.

Svenska riksrådets protokoll, iii, 58

(*c*)

7 July 1634. [The Peasants' Committee, who brought up their schedule of grievances, was called in to the Council-chamber and addressed by Herr Per Baner] who told them that the government had looked over their list of complaints, and was at a loss to understand what could have induced them to put in so ill-considered a memorandum, with its threat to go home immediately if they did not get their business despatched without delay. It was against all custom to mix their grievances up in that way with the answer to the Proposition. And the government had expected that they would have known better, particularly since this Diet is of importance, and concerns the welfare of the whole kingdom, and not least that of themselves and their children.

He accordingly urged them to settle upon a well-considered and decent answer, as has always been customary in the past. For they had not come there to bring up their grievances and complaints, but to deliberate, in conjunction with the other Estates, how the country might be placed in a position of security and prosperity. . . .

Svenska riksrådets protokoll, iv, 144

(*d*)

10 November 1635. [On the question of whether to continue the mill-toll]

Herr Per Baner: If we make concessions, or abolish any impost, the crown must somehow be supplied by some other means, either by resuming the lands which have been given away, or otherwise. A clause in the law of the land lays it down that if it should happen that any King diminish the crown's revenues, so that the King cannot live of his own, then his successor is entitled to annul his actions.

. . . .

Johannes Rudbeckius [bishop of Västerås] Reminded them of what befell the Roman Republic, how the constitution was overthrown by the keeping up of great armies, which led to internal dissension, and broke out in dangerous seditions. When the country is at peace again (said the bishop), the tolls can be removed. And said that the Clergy had certainly understood that the mill-toll was granted as a war-aid.

. . . .

Herr Per Baner: If anyone were going to complain of the mill-toll, the government would have expected it to be the Nobility, who have never been liable to taxation. And since there is no Estate which has not received great benefits from his late Majesty, if they are now going to refuse these aids the crown will be forced to revoke all those benefits which every Estate, and every private person, has received from it. The late King made handsome contributions to the University, to churches, and to schools: if the mill-toll were abolished, these would all have to be revoked by the crown.

Arosiensis [i.e. Rudbeckius, bishop of Västerås]: It is a matter of indifference to the Clergy whether the word *ordinary* [i.e. the statement that the mill-toll was an 'ordinary', and not an 'extraordinary', tax] be inserted in the Resolution or not; for the Estates cannot be tied so strictly by their own resolutions that they are bound to them for ever:

should the welfare of the country demand that a resolution be altered, they reserve to themselves the right to alter it. The power and authority which entitles them to make resolutions entitles them also to change them when the times demand it.

Ibid., v, 290-4

B

The Attitude of the Council

(*e*)

[From the Minutes of the Council]

1 September 1635. Discussion about a Diet, and debated whether it was necessary that all the Estates be called together, or only a strong committee, according to the tenour of the Form of Government, and that afterwards a good deal could be done with the peasantry about continuing supplies for the war by means of persuasion, either by a member of the Council, or by the local bishop.

. . . . . .

2 September 1635. Spoke again about the Diet; and it seemed that it would be best that all the Estates be summoned, since things of great importance were to be brought forward, and we should be deliberating about peace or war.

. . . . . .

5 September 1635. *Item*, it was finally decided that a general Diet be held on 8 or 10 October. There were indeed a number of cogent reasons for calling a general Diet, especially that the decision on war and peace lies in the sovereign *with the consent of all the Estates of the Realm*; next, that a province was to be restored to Poland, which is not only a matter of great importance, but since it was conquered with the aid of all the Estates, the approval of them all was required for its retrocession. Besides, the peace-commissioners will undoubtedly have arrived home by that time, and may then appear in person before the Estates, and explain to them all the reasons why it has been necessary to hand back Prussia.

. . . . . .

17 October 1635. Discussed whether the Estates ought to ratify the truce [of Stuhmsdorf with Poland]. It was argued that the King ought to ratify it with the Estates' approval.

Herr Johan Skytte said that in King Gustav's Testament [1560] it was stated that without the agreement and consent of the Estates the King ought not to make any law, give away any province, or conclude peace or any important alliance.

Count Per Brahe said at last that we must by all means uphold both the rights of the crown and the rights of the Estates, so that neither sustain any prejudice or infringement.

. . . .

21 October 1635. *Herr Per Baner* argued that the Estates were not directly to conclude, approve or ratify the terms of the truce which had been agreed to by the Commissioners, but they approve it in virtue of the fact that they subscribe the resolution of the Diet, since this was the express purpose for which the Diet was summoned, and since the Commissioners had previously been given full powers by the Regency to treat with Poland. . . .

Svenska riksrådets protokoll, v, 162–3, 166, 208–9, 213

(*f*)

20 July 1636. *The Steward* raised the point whether we ought not now to discuss with the Estates the possibility of a levy for the militia. . . . Or if we ought not perhaps to think of imposing heavier taxes instead.

The Chancellor [Axel Oxenstierna]: To what end, then, have you convoked the Estates, if you haven't agreed among yourselves about what you are to propose to them? Are they assembled simply to hear you engage in a discussion?

The Steward: We wanted to talk to them about the affairs of Germany; and we thought that if matters took an unforeseen turn, we could get their views on the situation.

The Chancellor: That will never do! You've got to paint Hell black for them, and make things out worse than they are – taking care, of course, not to make them so bad that they lose heart. . . . When a government fails to speak for the country and show a regal temper, but behaves like a private individual and champions the interests of the Estates, then that government cannot stand. . . .

Count Per Brahe: If the war is to continue, there will have to be a militia-levy. We only asked, since the people will have to be consulted, whether the question is to be put to them at a Diet beforehand, or whether we negotiate with them afterwards on a local basis.

The Chancellor: There have been a hundred militia-levies raised without any Diet's being called to consult with the peasantry about it. . . . As to taxes, there is nothing to be said about them to the Estates, except to tell them what they are to pay, and to exhort those who are present to see to it that those who are absent acquiesce. . . .

Ibid., vi, 445-7

(*g*)

23 September 1641. Thereafter *The Chancellor* suggested that seeing that the period for which subsidies had been granted by the Estates at the previous Diet is running out, not to mention the fact that he intends to spend a few weeks on his estates, they ought now to consider whether . . . the necessities of the country do not require the summoning of a Diet. . . .

As to the first point, *Herr Per Baner* remarked that such meetings of the Diet are a burden to the country; they entail a great deal of travelling and much expense for those who attend them. He thought therefore that it would be better, if such important matters should arise, that commissioners should be sent out to treat with the commonalty about them.

The Chancellor retorted: 1. That such commissioners cannot be arranged for without imposing a burden on the country. 2. Managing the people is difficult enough as it is. 3. It is not advisable to impose any tax on them without a Diet, since no King has ever ventured to do that, well knowing that the liberty of the Estates and Orders of the kingdom consists in a free grant, and in this it is reasonable to maintain them. 4. Besides which, we shall have to negotiate with the Nobility about the Customs.

Which arguments were approved by the others of the Council.

Ibid., viii, 719

(*h*)

8 January 1642. *The Chancellor* said that they must consider whether they were bound to communicate all alliances to the Estates. . . . Whether we do it as a matter of the law of the land, or for the public interest, that is the real question. If we consult and inform the Estates,

either we do it as an act of courtesy, or as a matter of necessity. If from necessity, and as a matter of law, then there must be something in the law of Sweden about it; but there is nothing of the kind. . . .

The Steward, Herr Per Brahe, considered that in general they should be informed, as a thing necessary and useful, for the following reasons: 1. Because we can collect from history, as well as from law, that former Kings laid the state of the country before the Estates; 2. just as the King may make no new law without the knowledge and consent of the Estates, so it seems reasonable that we inform them of treaties, which bind us to peace with our friends and hostility to our enemies, and this may involve the lives and resources of the subjects . . .; 3. the example of the late King Gustav [Adolf], who did nothing without the Council's counsel, and made himself loved and respected thereby.

Against the last argument it was objected that the late King often took the opinion of the Council and the Estates less from necessity than with a view to not appearing to be responsible for any disaster that might ensue.

. . . .

The Chancellor . . . was prepared to admit that nothing should be done without consideration by the Council; but ought it to be communicated to the other Estates? Although King Karl [IX] referred everything to the [Estates], it was to be expected that things would be different now from what they had been in those troubled times.

The Treasurer agreed with *The Steward*; but in order not to bind succeeding Kings by a precedent thought that we ought to include in the resolution a statement that the information was being given on this occasion only. But for special reasons this was not approved.

And since all members of the Council agreed that the Estates should be informed of the alliance [with the Dutch], especially, 1. because by consenting to it the Estates would bind themselves to assistance in terms of the treaty, and so would be unable later to argue that they knew nothing about it, and could therefore refuse to undertake to give aid regardless of circumstances; 2. because it was usual under previous Kings; 3. and is now more prudent for the Regency, who are the King's representatives; 4. because it puts the Estates in a good humour; 5. and, as *The Steward* and *Herr Johan Skytte* earlier argued, the King is more or less bound to it, by analogy. . . .

Ibid., ix, 15–17

VII-VIII

At the end of Oxenstierna's period in Germany there had been signs that his colleagues at home had lost confidence in his policies, and perhaps in himself. His return in the summer of 1636 dissipated these doubts and had a tonic effect upon the government. The Chancellor's force of character, his European prestige, his immense experience, his imperturbable self-confidence, his tireless attention to business, and his transcendent administrative ability, put him, within a few days of his arrival, in the position of unchallenged head of the government, a monarch in all but name. In Document **VII** he is to be seen steamrollering his political adversary Johan Skytte, asserting the principle of ministerial solidarity, and giving classic expression to the doctrine of the Council's function as regulator of the machine of state. In Document **VIII** he descends into the parliamentary arena, takes charge of the debate (quite eclipsing the Marshal of the Nobility) and by sheer force of personality beats down a solid opposition, and reverses an unanimous decision. It was no wonder if his enemies felt that his behaviour was overbearing, and resented it (**IX**).

VII Oxenstierna and the Council, 1636

Minutes of the Council of the Realm

26 August. It was ordered that the resolution of the Council be presented to Herr Johan Skytte for signature.

Herr Johan Skytte excused himself, and protested that he could not sign the resolution concerning the separation of their Majesties [i.e. the resolution that Christina was to be brought up apart from her mother], since he was not present when the matter was discussed and the vote taken, and had as yet had no opportunity to express his opinion. He entirely approved of the intentions of the Regency and the Council, and thought that it was commendable that they should be so solicitous for Her Majesty's proper education.

The Chancellor: This is not a question which is now moved for the first time: it was discussed many times before I came home. When the Regents and Council take a resolution, and somebody who has not been there comes forward afterwards and complains, and refuses to sign the resolution because he was not present when it was taken, he thereby reopens the whole question. We are Senators of this kingdom, and ought to stand as mediators between King and subjects, and speak not only for the rights of the crown, but for the law of the land and the due liberties of the country. It may be odious to the monarch, but it is required of us in virtue of the office we hold. . . .

Herr Johan Skytte: I want first to give my views and state my reasons.

The Chancellor: To that there can be no objection. Either your reasons will endorse or controvert our policy. If we find them to be so cogent that they prevail over our own reasons, then we will rescind our resolution; if not, the office of Counsellor of the Realm imposes an obligation upon him who holds it to sign all resolutions.

Svenska riksrådets protokoll, vi, 582–3

VIII Oxenstierna and the Estates, 1642

The Government had asked for the abolition of *skjutsning* and *gästning* (i.e. the obligation to convey, and to lodge, travellers on official business, and soldiers), and its replacement by a monetary payment. The proposal was debated by the Nobility on 26 January.

Minutes of the Estate of Nobility

After lengthy discussion it was unanimously agreed to grant, on behalf of their tenants . . . one silver *daler* from every full-sized farm, and proportionably from lesser farms, or one half of what is paid by crown-peasants and freeholders, and that their manors, and the home-farms attached to them, as well as land newly brought into cultivation, shall not be liable. . . .

On 27 January a committee of the Nobility went up to the Council to discuss this and other matters. On their return:

Herr Fredrik Stenbock reported that His Excellency [The Chancellor: Axel Oxenstierna] had explained to them at length that one silver *daler* would not be sufficient from the Nobility: they should think of giving six marks. . . .

On the 28th the Marshal of the Diet (Erik Gyllenstierna) drew their attention to the Chancellor's views

. . . and invited them, as true patriots, to consider the needs of the country, and not boggle at insignificant differences.

Long debates on this. At last all three Classes[1] resolved to stick to their first determination, seeing that the peasants were too poor, and money too short in various parts of the country, for the contribution to be increased.

On the following day

The Marshal said that having spoken yesterday with the Government, they had been informed that the aid given by the Nobility would not be adequate unless they raised it by another half-*daler*.

To this it was replied: That they had come to a unanimous decision, and could not go back on it.

The Marshal said that they were not being asked to go back on it but to add something to it.

To which all three Classes answered that they would stick to what they had agreed upon, and could not make any alteration now, since it would be intolerable for the peasants to contribute more.

The Marshal said: The Chancellor will be coming shortly, with some other members of the Council: you had better be prepared to defend yourselves and tell him why you can't do more.

Whereupon the Chancellor, *Herr Axel Oxenstierna*, arrived with *Major-General Lars Kagg*. And as soon as they had taken their proper seats, *The Marshal* expressed his humblest thanks that they had been at the trouble of coming here to communicate Her Majesty's pleasure to them. . . .

The Chancellor, acknowledging this, thanked them for their generosity in the past, and expressed the hope that their response would be similar in future, since the state was in great need of assistance.

Thereupon the Secretary read the draft answer to the Government's proposals.

When *The Chancellor* had heard it, he said . . . As regards the first point, there is something in what you say; but when you consider what disbursements are to be made out of the revenue arising from this source – to governors, bailiffs, bailiffs' men, and others who have to collect the taxes, as well in regard to the couriers of foreign ambassa-

[1] By the Ordinance establishing the House of Nobility (1626) the Nobility was divided into three classes, each with one corporative vote. Class I comprised Counts and Barons; Class II, persons whose ancestors had sat in the Council; Class III, the remainder of the Nobility.

dors, and the despatch of government business – you must see that we need considerable sums. . . . We of the government could of course leave things as they are, but the damage which would follow if we did forces us to try to find some other method to replace the burden of *gästning* and *skjutsning*.

This is a matter in which we must not look so much to our privileges, as to the welfare of the community; and if the community suffers, then I am afraid our privileges will suffer too; though it is of course quite right to try to safeguard them, and we have every reason to be grateful to the late King for respecting them. All sorts of evasions are practised to escape *gästning* and *skjutsning*: there are plenty of men who lump together the land they have inherited, the land they buy, the land they acquire by exchange, and then stick two huts, a barn and a stable on it and call it a manor, and so get themselves exempt. Can this be right? Judge for yourselves. Make no mistake about it, we don't intend that this sort of thing shall go on: if the system is useless to the government it will be abolished; and if you won't stand that, you may amend it yourselves. And anyway, what is half a silver *daler* to what you have agreed to already: it is we [of the government] who have to do the really difficult job of getting the Peasants to accept it. . . . So take a decision suitable to your privileges, like gentlemen and patriots; and act like noblemen, and not like a lot of peasants.

The Marshal invited them to bear in mind what the *Chancellor* had said, and come to decision by taking a vote.

Resistance immediately collapsed, and all three Classes proceeded without delay to vote the extra half-*daler*.

The Chancellor expressed his thanks to all the members for their public spirit in responding to his explanation so readily and with such generosity. . . .

He then urged them all to observe the provisions of the *Riddarhus*-Ordinance [1626] when voting in divisions, and not to behave like peasants . . . in the local court, so that the Marshal has to be constantly using his staff, just as the bailiff has always to be hammering on the table; but to remember in their debates that they are noblemen, and to allow one member of each family to talk at a time, so that the secretary can take proper minutes; and not to do as happens in the Polish Diet, where one member says 'Write this', and then another gets up and says 'Write that', and so one after the other until at last someone says 'Tear the whole thing up', and they go away no better than they came: but try to get a unanimous resolution on what you want to do. . . .

Thereupon the Chancellor took his departure.

And when the members who had accompanied him to his carriage returned to the House

The Marshal said: Gentlemen have no doubt grasped the point of what the Chancellor has been saying. And I confess to some considerable surprise that there was not a single member who ventured to answer him, although on other occasions there are some of you who do not seem to be lacking in self-confidence. But when it comes to the pinch, nobody is prepared to step forward. . . . Another time such persons will perhaps keep silent, and refrain from unnecessary speeches which they are not prepared to defend when occasion arises. . . .

Sveriges ridderskaps och adels riksdagsprotokoll, iii, 205-12

IX The Programme of the Opposition, 1647

Throughout the period of the regency for Christina (1632-44) there existed a party which mistrusted the intentions of the Regents and the high aristocracy, and feared some sort of aristocratic revolution at the expense of the monarchy. This party was led by Karl IX's illegitimate son, Karl Karlsson Gyllenhielm, and by Karl IX's son-in-law, the Count-Palatine Johann Kasimir, whose son was to become Karl X Gustav. It was supported by some rising men of middle-class origin such as Lars Grubbe and Nils Tungel, both now secretaries of state, by the Skyttes and their friends, and by all who were jealous or mistrustful of the dominance of the Oxenstierna family. Eventually it may be said to have included the Queen herself. In the early forties it was in questionable relations with the Danish minister, Peder Vibe. The following piece was almost certainly written by Karl Karlsson Gyllenhielm. It appeared anonymously, and in spite of purporting to speak for a majority was obviously concerned to take the popular line where possible in order to rally support; and this makes all the more significant its demands for some sort of popular or parliamentary control of ministerial appointments (§2:cf. **VI**(*a*)), and its claim for parliamentary supervision of expenditure (§6). The remainder of §2 refers to the undeniable fact that there were in 1647 four members of the Oxenstierna family in the Council. The demand for freedom of speech in parliament in §10 reflects resentment at Oxenstierna's authoritative exploitation of the means of verbal persuasion afforded by the *riksdag*-Ordinance of 1617 (**VIII**). The last clause (§15) is an attempt to mobilize opinion for a Palatine succession.

Remarks upon the Form of Government; by some good Patriots, being also a majority of the Estates
[1647]

At the last meeting of the Diet, on the occasion of our most gracious Queen's attaining of her majority and assuming the government, Her Majesty caused the Form of Government to be delivered over to the Estates for their further scrutiny, that they might consider whether it is to be confirmed as it stands, or after amendment. And the greater part of the Estates, having discussed it among themselves, offer the following observations upon it:

1. That as the Form of Government was instituted and prescribed by his late Majesty King Gustav Adolf (of glorious memory), and afterwards accepted and sworn to by the Estates of the Realm at a general Diet, to the end that . . . harmony, love and unity should prevail between all the Estates, and an orderly government be established according to the laws and statutes of Sweden, wherein the majesty of the crown, the authority of the Council, and the due rights and liberties of the Estates should be properly preserved to them, and thus (in particular) that no one element alone should draw all the power to itself, to the prejudice of an absent, ill, or minor sovereign; therefore we offer our most grateful thanks to God, that during Her Majesty's minority the Regency has remained so united in fruitful service of crown and country, until this time, when Her Majesty is now . . . come to the age when she may assume the government.

2. But as we have many instances from former ages . . . of how from ambition, selfishness, jealousy and ill-will not only a single man but also a single family or a single Estate has striven to exalt themselves and lord it over the rest, and when afterwards any attempt was made . . . to oppose this development, the consequence was unrest and public disturbance; therefore, in order to safeguard our posterity against this possibility (as far as human prudence can do) it seems to us that it may be well that in such cases no one shall be admitted a member of the Regency, or appointed head of one of the five Colleges, except by the following procedure: for each College the Estates shall first choose three names, and the King then choose which of them he pleases. . . .

If however there be no King of full age, then that the entire Council as then existing shall vote upon the three names proposed, and if their votes should be evenly divided between the three, then the choice shall be decided by lot....

And good care should be taken that (as is laid down in that clause of the Municipal Law which deals with brothers and relations on town-councils) there be not too many of the same family; for if it is undesirable to have too great a number of relations on a town-council, how much more should we be careful for the whole kingdom, in which all towns, and indeed all Estates, are concerned.

3. [And to the same end] those other high officers of the crown whom it must needs employ in the various provinces,... should also be elected and appointed with the goodwill and approval of the subjects who live in the district which they are to govern.

4. Next, that the same person should not serve more than one office, and thus draw double pay, but that others may have a chance of office and Her Majesty and the crown thereby be the better served.

5. And that no more offices be filled, or officers appointed, than is necessary; so that expense may be spared.

6. That every College and public office (not excluding the Council of the Realm) is bound, according to §38 of the Form of Government, to give an account of its proceedings at the time appointed by law. And if it should happen that Her Majesty or her great officers are prevented for weighty reasons from undertaking this work, or have no time for it, then other experienced men and good patriots should be appointed by the Estates to do it, so that the proper time for it be not suffered to pass; for it seems but just that the Estates, who contribute to the welfare of the kingdom, should know how their money is spent by those who have the handling of it, and that some do not get too much, and some none at all: there are complaints about this, and enquiries as to what the Form of Government lays down in this regard. The Estates therefore all humbly pray that Her Majesty, with the Council of the Realm, will be most graciously pleased to overhaul the list of office-holders, so that the superfluous officials, and the many foreigners who enter the country and are not essentially necessary to its service, may be struck off, and unnecessary expense be spared; seeing that the revenues are now considerably diminished by reason of the poverty of the people, and because so much crown land has been sold, or granted out as fiefs.

7. [Demand for better accessibility of justice in the provinces]

8. [Provincial officials ought not to put pressure on the courts to decide cases according to their wishes.]

. . . .

10. As to the right and liberty of the Estate of the Nobility to cast their votes freely and unconstrained, they well know that our late King (of glorious memory) established and affirmed it, in order that the Nobility might thereby be the more worthy of respect. And this being so, they would wish that they may not be treated in future as they have on occasion been treated in the past, when certain High Personages (whom they forbear to name or complain of, from the respect which they bear to the sovereign, as well as to those Personages and their offices) have snubbed the Nobility and assailed them with injurious words because some did not vote as they desired (**VIII**), and have refused to listen to the grievances of the Estate, and especially of its poorer members: a precedent which may well bring much evil in the future, as conducing to an infringement of their liberties and privileges. And therefore they humbly desire . . . that the Nobility may select three persons, not self-seeking or ambitious, but of good inclination to the Estate and to the fatherland, of whom whichever Her Majesty may be pleased to choose, may be named Marshal of the Nobility; and after the lapse of three years (or less, if the choice prove defective) . . . three others be duly put forward, and another chosen.

. . . .

15. . . . They are of opinion that we ought always to bear in mind the Form of Government's description of hereditary succession to the crown as being sounder and safer than the turbulence of electoral monarchy . . . and it is accordingly the earnest desire and humble dutiful request of all the Estates, that Her Majesty . . . will turn her mind to entering upon the estate of matrimony, according to the resolution of the Norrköping Diet [of 1604] . . . and be graciously pleased to declare herself to the Estates on this topic at this present Diet. . . .

The Estates [also] earnestly desire that Her Majesty may be pleased, while she is still in full health, to make definite choice of a successor [against the event of her dying without heirs] from the nearest collateral branch, with the consent of the Council of the Realm and the Estates, though without prejudice to her own rights or those of her heirs, if she should be blessed with any.

printed in *Svenska ridderskaps och adels riksdagsprotokoll*, iii, 409–16

X Constitutional issues at the Diet of 1650

The social crisis which came to a head at the Diet of 1650 (**XXIV, XXV**) had important constitutional overtones. For the first time the lower Estates, led by the Burghers and Clergy, seized the parliamentary initiative. They formed a common front to press for a Reduction, and concerted parliamentary manoeuvres between themselves, by exchange of deputations and joint meetings, in a way which had no precedent. The extracts printed below, from an imaginary *Conversation between Sir Peter, Parson Hans, Nils the Burgher and Jack the Yeoman*, reflect the sense of shock and outrage felt by the Nobility at these proceedings. It was written by Schering Rosenhane, who had observed the Fronde at close quarters, and feared that a similar upheaval might take place in Sweden. His main targets are the Clergy and the Burghers: *Jack the Yeoman* gets off lightly, as having been misled by the others. And as might be expected *Sir Peter* (the nobleman) is made to have the best of the argument on all points. The question whether the votes of a majority of Estates were to prevail over that of a single Estate here emerges as a serious issue for the first time since Gustav Adolf's *riksdag*-Ordinance (**II**), which had evaded the question by placing in the hands of the King the right to choose the opinion he thought best: it was to arise again in Karl XI's time, and again (in acute form) in the 1760s. To safeguard themselves against being voted down by a compact non-noble majority the Estate of Nobility tried (though never with success) to establish the doctrine that they had a *votum decisivum* which must in the last resort prevail (extract (*b*)).

(*a*)

Sir Peter: My dear Parson Hans, you grow hot without reason, for you understand not rightly what I mean. I do not deny that you are a free Estate, and that you ought to have your say at the Diet; and for so long as you made a proper use of your right, and gave a modest answer to that which your sovereign propounded to you (in so far as your Estate was concerned in it), and strengthened the other Estates in unity and obedience, you did yourselves honour, and deserved thanks; but when you aspire to take upon yourselves the direction of affairs, dragging the other Estates after you, and when you offer advice and make proposals unsolicited, and in matters which do not concern you, then I must say that a plain sermon, or a verse or two from God's Word, would come much better from your lips, than all the politics you can collect from Machiavelli, Campanella, Clapmarius, and others of the same kidney whom your brethren have begun to trail after them when they come to the Diet, and by whose principles you imagine the whole state is to be reformed. . . . But since you have appealed to these two honest fellows here, I am content to give them an opportunity to tell us what they think of it.

Jack the Yeoman: Well, Parson Hans, there is little I can say upon this head, being somewhat above my understanding; but there is an old proverb that the Clergy shall turn the whole world upside-down, and it is a common saying that when the parson will have one foot in the pulpit and another in the council-chamber, then no good will come of it . . . : we are but simple folk, and well content to remain so, and not to bother our heads with such high matters, but rather leave them to our sovereign, who cares for us all. It is true that at this Diet we have heard many secrets and many strange counsels, the like of which I never heard before; and sure never were peasants so wise as they are now become. And we have good cause to render thanks to the gentlemen of the Clergy for it, who have instructed us and opened our eyes, both through the sermons they delivered, and by other advices and timely informations, so that we may indeed confess that we had never come so far without them; but by what lights they were guided God knows: at former Diets the Clergy were not wont to be so wise – or so bold.

Nils the Burgher: You do not want words, Jack, and good words too for the Clergy; and there may be reason in what you say . . . but it seems to me that you forget our Estate of Burghers, and the aid you have had of us; and you should consider that the Clergy had never got so far in your business . . . had we not helped them and supported them like honest men. And you may be sure that though we are not so book-learned as they, yet we know what o'clock it is too: indeed, we have a man to speak for us who knows what he is about, I can tell you; and he can uncover such secrets, and cares so much for the welfare of us all, and has such weighty counsels and deep policies, that it were to be wished that the government would give ear to him, and then you would see how we should put things on a different footing. And although as yet we have not been able to do it, we have made such a beginning, and left such a Protestation behind us (**XXIV**), as to make it clear that we are concerned for the country's good, and that we have the power to make decisions about it when we please. If you good men of the Commonalty will but stick to us and the Clergy, you will see that you will have it in your power to be quit of taxes. You followed us pretty closely this time, and I do not think you will have lost by it; if you continue in that way, I hope that we shall come to a better condition.

Sir Peter: Good God, what words are these! Is it possible that such ideas and such proposals should be uttered by sane and rational men in a Christian country! . . . What do you mean by a better condition, and a different footing? Thank God for the footing we have, and the condition we enjoy! . . . All violent mutations and alterations in the affairs of government are attended by fearful dangers. Better in the meantime to suffer some abuses, especially if they be old and deep-rooted, and such as entail no great damage, than to be constantly teased with novelties and daily alterations; which in this case are the more to be feared since I see that you are altogether upon the wrong road, and running into danger. For you have got it into your heads to have recourse to remedies which are a thousand times more dangerous than the disease, touching as they do the fundamentals of government. If we consider what Nils Andersson said a moment ago, of secrets, and deep policies, and protestations, and how Clergy, Burghers and Peasants ought to stick together, and that it lay in their power to make changes; or if we regard the way they put these principles into practice at the Diet, and organized joint conventicles of the Estates, and how they discussed not what was proposed to them by the sovereign, but rather such matters as came into their own heads . . . – what are all such performances, if not what in other countries is wont to be accounted intolerable, and tantamount to the beginnings of sedition?

Parson Hans: One moment, Sir Peter! I must be allowed a word at this point, for you go too far. We cannot suffer you to put so false a construction upon our meetings, nor so distort what was so well intended. It is true that when we found any abuses or disorders in the government, then Clergy, Burghers and Peasants took counsel together and did what they could to correct them; and there may have been good reasons why we did not always invite the collaboration of the Nobility. And we do not think that the remedy we suggested was so absurd as you account it to be. And for the rest I would have you know that we are a free Estate, in attendance at a free Diet, and entitled to a free vote and free debate – to the same liberties, in short, as you are wont to enjoy.

Sir Peter: I wonder at you, Parson Hans, who are reputed a man of sense and learning, that you should so confound different things, and answer so unadvisedly. There is no question between us as to the right of the Estates to freedom of vote and debate at meetings of the Diet: I am not so ignorant as to dispute the point. But I will maintain, and do insist, that such a method of proceeding as you have adopted at this Diet becomes neither you nor any other Estate, if things are to be properly conducted; for before any debate or vote can be held it is essential that a matter be duly proposed for discussion by those who have the supreme voice in the nation's affairs; and our liberty consists in voting upon matters upon which our opinion is required. But liberty as you understand it is a liberty to direct policy, to propose among yourselves the matters for decision, to give advice, to launch a mass of innovations, to peer into *arcana status* (which are none of your business), and to conclude pacts between some Estates and exclude others from them. Such things are not comprehended in the idea of freedom of debate, and are not to be usurped by any Estate, *salva Majestate Regia*; for if this were once admitted, there would be no need for any minister or leader among you, and perhaps no King neither....

Nils: I cannot see that there is much that can be laid to our charge: we followed the same procedure as was customary in the past. Her Majesty proposed the topics for discussion, and we gave the best answer we could upon them. We made no Proposition ourselves; and if we consulted together, it was no wonder; for at coronation-time there is much to be thought of which cannot conveniently be considered on other occasions.

Sir Peter: You may say so, Nils Andersson, but you know better; ... and to refresh your recollection I will give you but one example, which you cannot deny: as soon as the Diet was begun, and Her Majesty's Proposition had been read out, and the Nobility had sat down to consider what answer should be made to it (supposing that all the other Estates would do the same, as has been customary in the past), there came to the Nobility a deputation from your Estate ... which began to suggest a whole string of new and important proposals, affecting the whole government and *fundamenta status*, and demanded that the Nobility enter into discussions upon them; but as this appeared to the Nobility to be a very dubious and unusual suggestion, they found it best, and most suitable to the duty and obedience which they owe to their sovereign, to answer first (according to ancient usage) to the points Her Majesty had propounded, and afterwards to await what further matters she might be pleased to bring forward. But you will remember what answer was thereupon returned to us by your representatives; namely, that what Her Majesty had proposed to the Estates was of no particular importance, and demanded no long time for an answer. But these new matters were of greater urgency, and ought first to be considered; and since they had been under discussion at the close of the former Diet, we ought to begin upon them at this, and more to the same purpose. . . . And do you think that this was in accordance with former usage, as you have said? If this was not an infringement of the royal prerogative and authority, then I do not know what is. . . .

Parson Hans: I see clearly, Sir Peter, that your meaning is that the Estates ought not to discuss or pursue any other topic than such as may be laid before them by the sovereign, and that you would quite subject us to the arbitrage and direction of others; but . . . are we then to keep mum when we are put upon, and cloak our necessities in silence?

Sir Peter: That is another question, Parson Hans. It is not my meaning to make slaves of us, so that we should not be allowed to lay our necessities before the government; and for this purpose there are two methods open to us by which we can do it with decency and propriety: first, the sovereign is graciously pleased to ask our opinion on matters which concern the kingdom, . . . and we have then an opportunity to use our answer to give an account of our condition and our needs. And next, as to all other matters which may affect one Estate or another, they can be brought forward by way of petition, and as you know it has always been the custom for the Estates to set forth their grievances *supplicando*, after they have answered to the Proposition which the government has laid before them; and this has always been well taken, and determined according to the nature of the case. But to begin with grievances, and to attempt to take them before the government's Proposition, is in my opinion to put the cart before the horse; it is something out of due season; and it is not in accordance with our constitution. For although the German Estates have begun to usurp the Emperor's authority in this way at their Diets, that is a different sort of constitution from ours, and by such actions they have brought the Emperor to that condition, that his power consists only in grand titles, and more in a seeming than in realities; and how it has gone in England, since the Estates began upon the same fashion, is sufficiently manifest to us from the events of the past few years.

. . . .

Samtaal emellan Juncker Päär, Mäster Hans, Niels Andersson Borghare och Joen i Bergha Danneman . . . 1650, pp. 8-19

(*b*)

Sir Peter: I perceive that it is one of your assertions that at meetings of the Diet the Estate of Nobility tries to vote you down, and claims some sort of pre-eminence, or a right of final decision. But this is all a delusion, or a deliberate falsehood; for the Nobility, to judge from the proceedings of all Diets up to this time, have never claimed more, or had any more share in decisions, than any other of your Estates. . . . So too you go astray when you contend that plurality of votes as between the four Estates should be entitled to prevail, and that when three Estates take the same line the Nobility and the government must conform to it. In another sort of constitution it may do very well: but in a monarchy, and in this country, you will never find a King willing to concede it. We come to a Diet as loyal subjects, to counsel, speak and answer in matters which are laid before us; and in these matters we are to hold confidential communication with one another, until at last we place our decision in the hands of the King or Queen; but for some Estates to league together, and to seek by a majority of votes to lay down the law – this is a thing of grave consequence and serious implications: by such means the time may well come when you will vote a King from his sceptre and crown, and the Nobility from their honour and welfare; and what good will you have of that?

Ibid., pp. 48-9

XI Addition to the Form of Government, 1660

The Addition to the Form of Government was necessitated by the tender age of Karl XI on the death of his father, and the need to amend the arrangements of 1634 in some important particulars. The Nobility, or some of them, would undoubtedly have wished to make it the basis of a *permanent* constitutional arrangement (as many had feared the Form of Government of 1634 might turn out to be): on this matter their attitude had altered since 1634. Not so the attitude of the other Estates, whose refusal to agree to any arrangement extending beyond the King's minority now defeated the idea. Constitutionally, the significance of the document lies in the way in which the Nobility seized the parliamentary initiative, as the lower Estates had seized it in 1650; in the emphatic (and final) assertion of the Diet's position as the only legislative organ (§XVII); in the explicit claim that Diets should be called at least every three years; and above all in providing that during the minority (but as yet only then) appointments to the Regency or the great offices of state must have the approval of the Estates (*cf.* **VI**(*a*), above). This, however, was a provision designed not so much as a curb upon the prerogative, as upon the exclusive pretensions of the high aristocracy. The Addition is also a clear reflection of the growing social tension, not only between Estate and Estate, but between high aristocracy and low. The contents of §§III and VIII, in this respect, indicate the progress made by lower nobility and the non-noble Estates in asserting their point of view. The exclusion of any prince of the blood from the great offices of state was aimed at Karl X Gustav's brother Adolf Johan, whom he had appointed in his will to be Marshal. The Estates, by an exercise of parliamentary sovereignty which was to cost some of them dear twenty years later, had annulled the will, despite prolonged resistance by Clergy and Peasants, who supported the unattractive Adolf Johan because they imagined him to be their friend, since he was the enemy of the high aristocracy. The interests of the inferior nobility, and of the non-noble Estates (here united), in a continuing Reduction, secured the adoption of §XII. §XV, with its envisaging of clashes between Regents and Council (never important in Oxenstierna's time), was to prove prophetic (**XII**).

We, Hedvig Eleonora,[1] together with the undersigned, the Council and Estates of the Swedish realm . . . who are now assembled in this . . . present Diet, with full powers on behalf of ourselves and of our brothers at home . . . have now agreed and resolved: That the government of the realm during H.M.'s minority shall be conducted in H.M.'s name by the Queen Mother and the five great officers of state: that is, the Steward, Marshal, Admiral, Chancellor, and Treasurer: on the model and in the form of that which was instituted and assented to at the Diet of 1634 . . .; but since times may change, and the passing of the years may bring alterations in all branches of state business, and nothing can be so good in intention and so carefully defined as to be exempt from modification and correction with the passage of time: therefore since we have found that the aforesaid statute and ordinance [i.e. The Form of Government] is now in need of amendment in some essential parts of it, as also of some further explanation of points which are liable to be misunderstood; we have taken the aforesaid statute, gone through it point by point, and carefully considered it; and we have set down the following observations, which in future are to be accounted as of equal force and validity with the old Form of Government:

[1] The Queen-Mother, Karl X Gustav's widow.

I

Confirms the religious provisions of §1 of the Form of Government, adding exemption for diplomats and their staffs attending service in embassy chapels.

II

The succession as regulated in 1649 and 1650 is confirmed.

III

Amends §§4 and 5 of the Form of Government as follows:

Although that ordinance lays down that the Council shall be twenty-five in number, yet since that time the services required by the country have expanded as the territories of the crown have increased, and it is no longer possible to adhere to so low a figure. The King is therefore free to employ and appoint a greater number of persons as his counsellors, provided that the number does not exceed forty . . . including in that figure the five great officers. . . . And it has also been found expedient that no more than one member of any one family shall be employed in the regency, and in the five great offices; and in the Council not more than three of any one family, . . . and also not more than two brothers at the same time, and not more than one son simultaneously with his father. And if it should happen that one of the five great officers should die during the minority, and another should fall to be appointed, then all such things ought to be done in consultation with the Estates, and by acceptance of their proposals; bearing always in mind that no prince of the blood is ever to be employed in these positions, but only the nobility and gentry of the realm.

IV

With reference to §§7, 8, 10–17 of the Form of Government.

It has likewise been found prudent and expedient that the leading Colleges . . . retain their authority and dignity, and be staffed (according to the tenour of the ordinance) with proper persons selected from native-born Swedes of the Nobility, and also from other Estates in so far as that has been usual and the office may be appropriate to them; and that the principal affairs of the country be despatched and transacted through the said Colleges;

provided always, that one College shall not meddle in the affairs of another, nor presume to deal singly with matters common to all; and that nothing which is the proper business of all of the Colleges, or of one of them, be dealt with *extra collegium*, or in the absence of the College concerned; but that all the Colleges remain together in Stockholm, the next senior member presiding, should the president be absent. . . .

V-VI

Further regulation of procedures of the Supreme Court.

VII

The two new Colleges – of Trade, and of Mines – established during Christina's minority, to continue: Instructions for them should be drawn up.

VIII

Regulations for the Marshal, the Master of the Ordnance, the Master of the Horse, and the Master of the King's Hunt. These and other principal court officers

shall be filled by such members of the Nobility as are not members of the Council of the Realm; but the office of General-Governor [of the newly-acquired provinces] shall be filled without limitation of choice by persons drawn either from the Council or from the Nobility in general – provided, however, that no member of the Council be permitted to occupy more than one office in addition to his councillorship.

. . . .

And in all appointments to posts attention is to be paid to the capacities and merits of the candidates, so that no one be excluded simply on the ground of humble birth, nor advanced solely on the ground of social standing; and no person is to be permitted to cumulate more offices than such as necessarily go together, or than he is capable of discharging it being always understood that no nobleman may hold more than two. In particular, that no native Swede who is fit for a post be passed over in favour of a foreigner; provided however that meritorious and serviceable officers of foreign birth are not to be contemned or thrust aside. We reaffirm, moreover, as a general reservation, that no man who does good service is to be removed from his post (except for promotion) without good cause, or unless convicted of delinquency, except in those instances where an appointment has been made for a limited number of years. . . .

. . . .

XII

General approval of provisions regarding the army, the periodical inquisitions into the work of the Colleges, the summoning of Diets, naturalization of foreigners, duties and emoluments of office, etc.

In which connexion we have only this to observe: that if during the King's minority pressing reasons should make it impossible to avoid giving satisfaction to deserving persons, either by ennobling them, or by naturalizing them and conferring lands and favours upon them, that in such a case it be done as cautiously and sparingly as possible, and that (as in other matters of importance) steps be taken to secure the advice and consent of the Council; and that particular care be taken to see that those who are naturalized do not secure that privilege for the whole of their family, but only for their persons and their heirs, and that they be not at once allowed to hold any major office, or command any fortress, or have a share in the education of the King, and above all be not allowed to become members of the Council, which is to be composed only of native-born Swedish noblemen. And if the handing-out of lands and rewards should prove to be unavoidable, we submit that it should be done and regulated according to His late Majesty's statute and the resolution of the Diet of 1655 (**XXVI**), so the King and crown may have a hope of recovering them at some future time, and also the means to do so. . . . But if, in order to pay the genuine debts of the crown, or to repay straight loans, or to meet a non-recurrent crisis, the government is forced to pledge some of the crown estates, as has been usual in the past, then the terms of the transaction . . . ought to be honestly adhered to, so that no one is let down by relying on the government's promises. . . . It is a question which we recommend with the utmost urgency to the government and to those who manage the finances, that those who serve their King and country may receive such reasonable provision, by way of wages, that the nation's affairs shall be in no danger of stoppage or neglect by reason of their non-payment.

XIII

The annual examination of the records and accounts of the leading officers of government is endorsed, though it is accepted that (as in 1638) the pressure of other urgent business may prevent the Regents from doing it at the proper time.

XIV

Provisions for the Regency, as in the Form of Government §§ 52-end, endorsed, with the addition of the Queen-Mother to the Regents.

XV

. . . If it should happen that the six Regents cannot agree among themselves on any matter, they are to seek the advice and award of all members of the Council who are available. If the Regency should bypass the Council on the ground that it is unnecessary to notify them of a matter of small importance; and if any member of the Council, not being of the Regency, should have doubts about it, and in good faith desire to express his views on it, he may ask either the Queen-Mother or the Chancellor at the next Conference to call the Council together, when every member will be free to make such observations as may appear to him to be appropriate and necessary.

XVI

Acts of the Regency are in general provisional only, and subject to the King's confirmation at his majority.

XVII

Likewise whatever is resolved at a general Diet is to have the force of law, until the same has been ratified or annulled by the King, with the assent of the Estates, at another Diet. And although Diets may be something of a burden and an expense . . . yet it seems necessary, during H.M.'s minority, that they be not deferred for more than three years, but that the Estates come together every third year, that they may hear and understand what has passed concerning the kingdom and the government in the intervening period. . . .

XVIII

But if it should happen that matters arise which are of such importance that the Regents, even with the advice of such members of the Council as may be available, do not venture to deal with them, and time does not permit the summoning of a Diet, then if need be the Regents may avail themselves of the advice and opinions of such members of the five Colleges as ordinarily are resident in Stockholm. They are not in any event to summon any provincial meeting of the Estates; but if the matter cannot be resolved by the five great officers, and the ripe advice and opinions of the Colleges, then instead of a provincial gathering they are to summon a full Diet, and call together all the Estates of the realm.

XIX

Everything in the Form of Government not amended by this Addition is to retain the force of law.

E. Hildebrand, *Sveriges regeringsformer . . . samt konungaförsäkringar*, pp. 42–58.

XII The Regency and the Council, 1665

By the mid-1660s the possibility envisaged in §xv of the Addition to the Form of Government had become a fact. The Regents and the Council were at odds, and the remedy provided in §xv proved ineffective. Undoubtedly the Council tried to meddle in government to a greater extent than in Oxenstierna's time; and it was against this meddling that the petition of the Nobility, alluded to at the end of this document, was directed. The Council still regarded itself, as in 1611, as the guardian of the constitution against the encroachments of the prerogative, as a mediator between King and people, as *ephors*; and Clas Rålamb in this matter spoke much the same language as Erik Sparre, a century earlier. But though their number had been increased in 1660 to a maximum of 40, they still were mostly drawn from the narrow circle of great families, and the lesser Nobility had grown jealous of their monopoly of the plums of office. Dislike of the Council's meddling was above all directed at their influence on appointments, and the petition represented the anger of lesser nobles who were desperate for government jobs. This urgent material consideration made the mass of the nobility lukewarm on the constitutional issue: unrestrained prerogative might well offer a better hope of advancement than monarchy limited by high-aristocratic control. Hence the nobility tended to support the Regents, as temporary representatives of the prerogative – and this despite the fact that it was the Regency's financial policies (as the Council saw) that jeopardized the payment of the wages of the state's servants. Hence too they defeated the Council's attempt, on Karl's attaining his majority in 1672, to impose on him a more stringent Charter than his father had given in 1654. Already the situation existed which was to make absolutism possible after 1680; and already the Council was alienated from the Estates.

Draft of a Memorial which the Council of the Realm intended to have delivered to the Regency . . . , containing certain observations on its administration of the Nation's affairs

[By Clas Rålamb]

After complaints about defective security for the King's person, and the inadequacy of his education, the Memorial proceeds to criticize the Regency's inconstant and changeable policies.

. . . We therefore urge that greater consistency, and less levity, be observed in the conduct of the nation's affairs; so that decisions taken at one moment by one section of the Regency and Council be not revoked later by another section; but that whenever it is obvious that there is a specific reason for a matter to be reconsidered, it be done in the presence of those who first took the decision.

There is no lack of good laws: what is lacking is their proper execution.

For there can scarcely be anything more prejudicial than carelessly and negligently to allow the commands of the sovereign to be flouted, and to suffer them to remain without effect. We say nothing of the consideration which ought to be given to the wishes and demands of the Estates, who, when the drafts of so many projected ordinances were put before them at the last Diet, desired that a proportion be deferred to their next meeting; yet they subsequently appeared in print notwithstanding, in contravention of the Form of Government of 1660. . . .

The lands of the crown have from time immemorial been intended to support the monarchy, and to supply other needs of the country . . . , and it has always been the practice to consider the rewarding of deserving persons as among those needs. When, however, this is done lavishly and recklessly, experience has shown that the result has been the profound perturbation of the Estates; as appears from . . . their supplication to Queen Christina in 1650 (**XXIV**), and the Statute of 1655 (**XXVI**). And as this last is designed for the correction of such disorders, it seems most necessary that the scope of the Reduction should be finalized, so that it may be brought to completion as originally intended, and the crown at long last be relieved of the burden of trying to find the money to pay the salaries of those in the Colleges . . . ; and, for the rest, that crown-lands, once recovered, should as far as possible be retained, . . . and not given away again save in case of real necessity. . . . Yet we hear every day that an estate is no sooner redeemed by the crown than it passes into the hands of somebody else, irrespective of where it may happen to be situated. Otherwise it is to be feared that the whole work of Reduction may come to such a pass, that instead of redressing the abuses which existed up to 1655 we may see affairs drifting into greater and greater confusion, and that His Majesty, when he assumes the government at his coming of age, may find that even inalienable places have not been left untouched. . . . We may remind you that the former Regency, which carried on the government in Queen Christina's time, exercised very great restraint in this matter: they gave donations of land only to a few exceptionally deserving persons; and they entirely neglected to reward themselves. . . .

The Memorial goes on to criticize excessive peer-creation and increasing abuse by the Nobility of the privileges of their order.

. . . In this way our privileges become intolerable to the crown; so that even though they may be based on rights going back for centuries, to time immemorial, they must in the end be overthrown, since they have reached a pitch at which they have become irreconcilable with the continued existence of the inalienable rights and revenues of the monarchy, and the maintenance of the armed forces of the kingdom; with the result that they must eventually come under constant attack by the other Estates, to the great harassment and distraction of the sovereign. This should be clear enough from what happened at the Diet of 1650 (**X**); and also from the mutterings which were heard among the commonalty at the Diet last year, to the effect that 'there will soon be as many nobles as peasants'. We therefore suggest to the Regents, in a spirit of friendly remonstrance, that they should consider whether this spring, . . . instead of further creations of peers, they might not try by appropriate means to stimulate the numerous younger members of the nobility to apply themselves to whatever type of training they may be best fitted for by nature and education, so that henceforward only those may be employed in the Civil Service who have acquired in their youth the knowledge and experience necessary to the discharge of their duties; and that the remainder apply themselves to military exercises. And as this is hardly to be achieved by mere words and exhortations, it would be well that the latter class of persons should be clearly cut off from all hope of employment in the Civil Service, unless or until they have won distinction in the military line either at home or in the service of a foreign prince; so that we may at long last have the satisfaction of being able to say that persons are selected to fit the job, rather than that the job is modified to fit the person (**XXVII**).

. . . .

We are at a loss to understand how it is that although in 1660 and 1661 the country was still in serious difficulties as a result of the disorder produced by the war, affairs were so managed that in the following year, 1662, it was possible not only to pay all the crown's servants their full wage (a thing which had not been done for many years previously) but also to put aside several *tunnor* of gold for paying off the crown's debts; whereas from that time forward there has been an ever-increasing stringency and shortage of money, despite the fact that in all succeeding years God blessed the country with peace and good harvests. If our affairs are to continue to be conducted in such a way that the budget cannot be balanced in peacetime, . . . we cannot conceive how it will be possible to justify such a record to His Majesty, and to the Estates of the Realm. . . .

We therefore consider it indispensably necessary that the situation be carefully reviewed, with a view to discovering the causes of this disorder, and the remedies for it, and that an effort be made to offset it by better management of the revenues of the country. We are not unmindful of the fact that from time to time the Exchequer has submitted representations on this head; but they have never been taken seriously enough for the Council to be invited to formulate resolutions upon them. And this is true not only of finance but of many other things also: for instance, in the granting of land, appointments to office, publication of ordinances and proclamations, and many other matters (some important, others not), the advice of the Council of the Realm has not been asked for, and policy has been determined by decisions taken by the Regents among themselves, or at most has been communicated to the Council simply by way of notification; though the law of the land, the Form of Government, and the sworn undertaking given by the Regents to the Estates, all require a very different procedure – to wit, that everything is to be enacted and decided with the advice and consent of the Council. But not only has this not been done, but if any member of the Council has ventured to offer a pertinent observation he has been either cut short before he could say the half of what he was minded to say, or met with hard words and contradictions. We find it difficult to form a conjecture as to the motives for this behaviour; but when we recall how a short while ago the Regents permitted a small minority of the Nobility to impugn the dignity and integrity of the Council, by means of a petition delivered to them privately after the close of the Diet – a petition which was read in haste . . . and never subsequently communicated to the Council as a whole, nor any opportunity afforded for the discussion of its very compromising allegations – then we can hardly fail to form the impression that this derogatory document must bear some responsibility for the effects which followed it. . . .

Printed in *Den svenska fatburen*, No. 7, 4 July 1769, pp. 105–19.

XIII An Italian's impressions of the Swedish constitution, 1674

Count Lorenzo Magalotti (1637–1712) was a Florentine diplomat and *littérateur*, who left extensive manuscript accounts of his visits to various parts of Europe. In 1671–4 he was in Flanders and England; went thence to the abortive peace-congress in Cologne; and from June to September of that year visited Sweden in a private capacity. His account is based on information collected during his visit, and on what he had learned from Swedes of his acquaintance before he arrived, and is in general remarkably accurate, for he was a quick and acute observer. His remarks on the constitutional position (extract (*a*)) present us, at almost the last possible moment, with a picture of the authority and influence of the Council as men like Clas Rålamb were anxious to keep it. His judgment on Karl XI was just for the time of which he was writing: no one could have foreseen how he would develop. Extract (*b*), with its linking of the possibility of absolutism in Sweden with the prevailing social unrest, is both penetrating and prophetic.

(*a*)

In the first place, as to Sweden's constitution in general – and by this

I mean its constitution as it really is, and not as it seems to be – I affirm it to be a pure aristocracy, disguised under the name of monarchy. . . . The government is thus not what it purports to be. The laws give to the Estates more power than they do in fact possess; the government is defective in that the King, despite the fact that his crown is hereditary, and that he is in control of the army, is more limited than he should be.

In reality, it is the Council which deprives the Estates of their lawful powers, and the King of his sovereign authority. The Council dominates the Estates under the appearance of acting as mediator between them and the crown; and dominates the King, as being the body with the right to advise him. And in virtue of their office the councillors are indeed both the one thing and the other – though they are not so in reality. The Council is no mediator, for it always constitutes itself the King's spokesman, and always tries to put the power of decision – and the property of the subjects – into his hands; and this with the idea of encouraging the King to believe that it does in fact play a mediating part, and of strengthening his belief that it is necessary to the monarchy, while at the same time creating or using a pretext to divide up the subjects' property among its members – for it is only when it comes into the King's treasury that they have a chance of getting their hands on it. Nor can one say that the Council really functions as a body of the King's advisers, since the tendency is for all things increasingly to conduce to the greatness, advantage, and power of that body – at whatever cost. It also uses its position as a body of official counsellors of the crown to hinder access to the sovereign's person to all those who, deriving no benefit from his subjection to its imagined authority, would therefore advise him in accordance with his real interests. If any ruler is to liberate the crown from this masked tyranny, he will need to be either born outside Sweden, or brought up in a foreign country before his accession. King Karl X Gustav, the present King's father, possessed both these advantages, and was therefore a King of a very different character. He always, in fact, did whatever he pleased; and since throughout his reign he had the country under arms, he was able to do so with impunity, though it never happened that he actually overstepped the law. If he had lived, however, he might perhaps have imparted this useful secret of success to his son. But Karl XI has had the ill-fortune to be brought up by guardians: admittedly guardians prescribed by law, but not appointed by royal authority. I take it, therefore, that his father's secret is always likely to elude him. Every care has been taken to avoid anything that could lead him to independence of thought or action. If he does discover the secret, it will be by accident.

The following short account, however, may give some idea of how things stand. As to the administration of the country, it remains enshrouded in a mystical cloak of countless formalities, . . . but to give some idea of it, I may say that the government seems to rest upon the assembly of Estates, which consists of Nobility, Clergy, Burghers and Peasants. Without their collaboration the King seems to be unable to raise taxes or make militia-levies, nor on his own responsibility can he decide on peace or war, or many other things of like nature. The outward show, with all its formalities, is so carefully preserved, that those who are the actors in the scene really believe themselves to be the characters they are playing, and never realize that they are participants in a comedy. All Kings are disposed to contend that they have greater rights over their subjects than those subjects are prepared to admit; and in the same spirit the King of Sweden insists that the Council can only advise, and not determine. The Council for its part denies this, pointing out that there would be no need for the King to collect their advice if he were not bound to follow it, especially when they happen to be unanimous. Disputes of this kind are perennial, although the Kings can usually produce good grounds for their contentions. But there are some things which the King cannot do without causing serious trouble. He cannot, for instance, levy soldiers [on his own authority]. . . . He cannot demand extraordinary contributions in kind, or money, without the assent of the Estates; he cannot have full control of the government until he has completed his twenty-fifth year; and finally he cannot be crowned without the Estates' permission. Nor does he, in fact, violate any of these rules. It is indeed impossible for the King not to pay a good deal of attention to the Council's opinions, since although he may appoint anyone he pleases to that body, he may not dismiss them, once he has nominated them. For although the people always hate the members of the Council for their pride, their pretensions, and their venality, still they love their laws too well to suffer them to be trampled under foot, even though the effect would be to hurt the Council's interest more than any other. . . .

The King, moreover, does not exercise only that authority which is incontrovertibly his. . . . He does much besides. And perhaps on careful examination it might be found that he does more than he has a right to do. For example, he concludes alliances with foreign powers; or alters the privileges of the towns; or starts a war. King X Gustav acted in this way when he began his second war against Denmark. He insisted that it was a necessary corollary of the former war, which had been begun with the Estates' consent – and this despite the fact that a Diet was actually being held in Göteborg at the time.

Lorenzo Magalotti: *Sverige under år 1674* (trans. C. M. Stenbock), pp. 2-3, 6-7.

(*b*)

It is . . . to be feared that the King of Sweden may succeed, with the help of the new nobility, in doing what the King of Denmark did with the help of the burghers, who hated the nobility and therefore lent themselves to his plan of freeing himself from dependence upon the Estates and making himself absolute. The same thing could occur in Sweden, where it might easily happen that the new nobility, which hates the old (from among whom, as a rule, the members of the Council are exclusively recruited) would unite with the King (upon whom they mostly depend) to destroy and abolish the power of the Council, and liberate the King from its yoke.

Ibid., p. 74

XIV The attack on the Regents and the Council, 1675

The Diet met in 1675 under the impression produced by the reverse at Fehrbellin, the danger from Denmark, the obvious lack of effective measures to defend the country, and the growing realization of the desperate financial position. For all these things the Estates blamed the former Regents, some of them still in office as ordinary members of the Council and heads of their respective Colleges. When asked to provide supplies the retort of the Estates was to present the Memorial from the Secret Committee which is printed as extract (*a*). The Council returned a shuffling answer, in which it tried to shelter itself behind the alleged consent of the Estates (extract (*b*)); who retorted by a direct appeal to the King (extract (*c*)). The King's reactions mark the beginning of a constitutional revolution. He had indeed, upon attaining his majority, given to his much-trusted uncle, Magnus de la Gardie, and his co-Regents, a full acquittance; but (as the Estates rightly supposed) he had never really examined their report: if he had, he would have noticed that the statistical appendices to it, to which frequent reference was made, had not in fact been appended, no doubt for the excellent reason that they would hardly have substantiated the Regents' account of themselves. The Estates now invited him to disavow his acquittance. The experiences of 1675 were rapidly disillusioning Karl with his uncle's *régime*; and he replied to the Diet's Memorial by giving the Estates leave to set up an investigating committee to look into the administration during the minority. Not only that: he gave the committee leave (extract (*d*)) to call for the minutes of the Council of the Realm, and of the Colleges, to provide them with evidence for their investigation. Here begins the system of examination by the Estates of the minutes of government offices which was to be so characteristic a feature of the Age of Liberty: the first example of a new device for ensuring ministerial responsibility to parliament. The Council itself was deeply divided between de la Gardie's supporters and his critics; and the latter faction, or some of them, were quick to dissociate themselves from the policies (or lack of policies) now under attack: this was soon to develop into an attempt to dissociate the Council as a whole from any share of responsibility for the Regents' actions (**XV**(*f*)). The investigating committee continued its work for the next five years: the upshot appeared at the Diet of 1680.

(*a*)

Minutes of the Estate of Nobility, 9 September 1675

After a meeting of the Secret Committee, it was resolved that the Committee should present to the Council of the Realm the following memorial:

. . . In the year 1672, while the last Diet was sitting in Stockholm, the Lords of the Council communicated to the Secret Committee the decision which they had reached about the international situation at that moment, and its effects upon the country's interests; and they represented their policy as being directed simply and solely at securing a general pacification, and in particular at eliminating any factor that might lead to the kindling of the flames of war in our own dear fatherland. The Estates then (as was their duty) expressed their thanks to H.M. and to the Council for this vigilant care for their interests, and came forward with a humble memorial in which they likewise urged that efforts be made to obtain a general peace, and above all that our dear fatherland be kept out of the war. Since that time, however, Their Excellencies of the Council have given their approval to the invasion of the territory of the Elector of Brandenburg by H.M. forces, though it might have been foreseen that such a step, however reasonable and justifiable it may have been, would give an opportunity and pretext to all H.M.'s ill-wishers to combine against him, and though even in the most favourable years the resources of this country must seem quite inadequate to resist the large forces which they can bring together. The Estates of the Realm cannot bring themselves to believe that the Lords of the Council were prepared to approve and advise an invasion of Brandenburg (the consequences of which must infallibly have been foreseen . . .) – without regard to the assurances given to the Estates, and without their knowledge – unless Their Excellencies were certain of having at their disposal the means, supplies and resources for the efficient conduct of the operation, independently of what the Estates might be prepared to contribute. And of this the Estates were the more assured, inasmuch as the Almighty has been pleased to vouchsafe to our fatherland fourteen years of much-needed peace, during which period (no doubt) such reserves have been accumulated as may be required for this large-scale enterprise, besides other means of which the Estates are ignorant, but which will doubtless be recommended to them; and they assume that when all this is drawn upon, and the Estates likewise give such aid as may be possible to them, H.M. will be in a position to deal with the difficulties which now confront him. And whereas His Majesty has been graciously pleased to reveal to the Estates the designs of his enemies, and has asked our aid and support in men and money; although it is their bounden duty as faithful subjects in such a case to come to H.M.'s assistance, and not to be backward in that which it becomes them to do; nevertheless, since they are still ignorant of the financial basis upon which Their Excellencies grounded and calculated their advice aforesaid, therefore the Estates deem it necessary that they receive full information of these things from Their Excellencies, so that they may then be in a better position to determine how much they ought to contribute, for the present purpose, by way of addition to existing resources.

Sveriges ridderskaps och adels riksdags protokoll, xii, 59–60

(*b*)

Extract from Minutes of the Council of the Realm, 15 September 1675

The Council of the Realm would have been glad to give an earlier reply to the extract from the Minutes [(*a*), above] delivered to them some days ago by the Secret Committee. This was, however, a question of such difficulty as to make that impossible, despite all their efforts; and the Council desire and expect that the Estates of the Realm will not fail to bear that in mind. As to the question itself, the Council have given due consideration to all the points in the communication that was made to them, and they find three in particular upon which the Estates desire an answer: 1. Why it has happened that the country has become involved in war, in contravention of the assurances given at the last Diet, and without previous communication with the Estates? And 2., on what financial basis the Council advised a rupture with Brandenburg? 3. That in the 14 years in which we have enjoyed peace, it is to be presumed that resources have been accumulated which are now available towards the cost of the war.

As to the first point, the Council answer that they flatter themselves that the Estates will remember that everything that passed at the last Diet was communicated to them in full, and was approved and endorsed by them through their Committee. Of all that has happened subsequently, up to the present moment, the Estates have been apprised by the full report made to their Committee at the Diet, by H.M.'s order; and they make no doubt that the Estates must certainly have noted that all our measures were shaped and designed to the maintenance of peace, as far as might be practicable (as may be verified from the official papers), and that everything that has passed since the last Diet is to be considered only as a corollary of what was previously communicated to them. The Council therefore take it for granted that nothing has been done without the knowledge of the Estates, although it was not practicable to convoke them in so sudden an emergency.

Concerning the second point, the same explanation applies; and the Council is well assured that they took into consideration all the contingencies of which the Estates now remind them, and all the consequences against which human foresight could provide; and to this their minutes, resolutions, and other public acts all bear witness.

The position in regard to the third point is that the Council must inform the Estates that at the time of H.M.'s happy assumption of the government the Council handed over to H.M. a full statement, written in a book, with a complete account of how the revenue was spent every year, as well as of everything else concerning their administration, and the appendices to that book, as well as the accounts in the Treasury, must make it clear what chance there was to save anything on the annual budget.

. . . .

Ibid., xii, 176

(*c*)

The Estates' Memorial to the King concerning the War with Brandenburg, the Regents' administration, etc. (endorsed: read before H.M. and the Council, 18 September 1675, at Uppsala)

After some days' delay the Council of State have been pleased to send us an answer [(*b*), above] in which they refer us, for the causes of the present war, to the consent which they pretend that we gave to their message to the Estates at the last Diet. As to their conduct of the administration during Y.M.'s minority, they appeal to the statement of accounts which they allege themselves to have presented to Y.M. upon your assuming the government. Be this as it may, it does not alter the fact that our main concern was to discover what means Their Excellencies may be supposed to have had in mind for carrying on a war which they had themselves advised; and we had hoped that Their Excellencies would have been in a position to enlighten us on this point. . . . We should have received the information with infinite satisfaction, since it would doubtless have revealed that upon the most careful calculation our resources had been judged to be fully equal to the carrying out of what we are engaged in. For we certainly were unwilling to suppose that it was intended that at a later stage – when the enterprise had become difficult and dangerous – the whole weight and burden of it was to be suffered to fall upon us alone.

As to the administration, which must bear the responsibility for our present wretched condition, our knowledge of it is no doubt limited to what is everywhere evident. If, therefore, Their Excellencies have indeed presented any accounts to Y.M., we are very ready to leave it to Y.M.'s own judgment; but we venture humbly to express our confident belief that Y.M. cannot have intended to give them his approval or discharge, except subject to the result of a subsequent and more careful scrutiny. We are not aware whether Y.M. was able to give yourself time to examine these accounts, and for that reason we remit the whole matter to Y.M.'s most gracious approbation; but if Y.M. should be unwilling to burden your exalted person with labour of this kind, we could wish that Y.M. might be graciously pleased to depute for this purpose certain persons drawn from the Estates, who would be able to check the accounts carefully....

For the rest, we had certainly supposed that we had explained to the Council with sufficient clarity that we were totally unaware of ever having given any sort of consent to the present war. But since we perceive that Their Excellencies place the whole responsibility for it upon the approbation of the Estates at the Diet of 1672, of which they allege the present complications to be the direct consequence, we can only say that if by this they understand our alliances, we recollect most clearly that the alliance-treaties had already been printed and published, and therefore could not have been further approved by us; and we find from the very wording of the Diet's resolution that we were purely and simply concerned with the preservation of the peace, and the security and defence of all the frontiers of the realm; and it is therefore out of the question that we should have approved any measures which had not that end in view. That same resolution also contained a very explicit recommendation that we should put ourselves in a good posture of defence: how well Y.M. has been served in this respect we cannot, of course, say.... In addition, we remember very well that when the alliances were read over to us, we were given all sorts of assurances that not only was this a policy that entailed no risks, but that it would conduce to the prestige, advantage and security of Y.M. and the country, since Y.M. would be enabled, by mediating between the belligerents, to retain control of events, and not be forced to burn his fingers to pull out chestnuts for somebody else: that, in short, it would enable you to keep the peace, and to confer upon your faithful subjects all those blessings which a peaceful existence brings with it. Compare this with the dangers in which Y.M. and every province of this realm are now involved, when Y.M. has been led step by step into a most onerous and dangerous war, not only with the Emperor, but with other potentates, whereby Y.M.'s ill-wishers have been given cause to forward their evil designs. And all this without our having any friendly naval power upon whom we can rely (which was plainly foreseen), and with a state of affairs at home which is now seen to be far worse than anyone could possibly have imagined, after 14 years of peace!

In view of all this it is no wonder if such things (and others too) appear to us to be matters of concern, or that so unusual a constellation of circumstances induces in us unusual reflections, being that the humble duty we own to Y.M., and the natural love of every man for his fatherland . . . oblige us not to relax our efforts, or forbear our remonstrances, until we are assured that as far as is humanly possible Y.M., the country, and the many thousands of souls who dwell therein, are by God's help in a condition to escape from their present dangerous predicament. . . .

Ibid., xii, 178

(*d*)

Minutes of the Estate of Nobility, 22 September 1675

The Marshal of the Nobility reported that a member of the Council had asked him how it was that now that the Nobility, together with the other Estates, had so strongly attacked the Council in their Memorial [(*c*), above], they stopped short and made no further effort of any sort; at which the Council felt called upon to protest.

Governor Henrik Falkenberg: And a member of the Council said to me, too: 'Why so slack now, when formerly you were so hot?' Since we have attacked the whole Council, they are pretty certain to hand in a protest against this Estate.

The Marshal: The Treasurer told me yesterday that the King is thinking of getting some of the Council to come down to us to obtain some decision about men and money; and that the Council is hard at work on an explanation of their reasons for the war. And that if the Nobility were still wanting to be allowed to see the Council minutes, H.M. was disposed to give them leave.

Herr Reutercrantz said that Secretary Olivekrans had orders to show us the Minutes.

Governor H. Falkenberg said that he could scarcely believe that the Council minutes would be brought down to the House of the Nobility; the Secret Committee would have to go up to the castle to read them.

The Marshal: The King is content that the Nobility should themselves appoint a committee to look at the finances. . . .

Herr Clas Fleming: The job will have to be done in Stockholm, for it will not be finished in a hurry.

The Marshal: What will be the best way to get at the accounts? The Treasury will have to give us information.

Governor Falkenberg: There is a narrative which was drawn up and handed over to H.M., and we can get some guidance from that, as well as from the reports drawn up by the Council in 1662 and 1668, which are in the Treasury.

The Marshal asked if the Estates' Secret Committee was also to look at the speeches and opinions of the Queen-Mother, as recorded in the minutes?

Governor Falkenberg thought not: all reports in the minutes of the Queen's remarks and votes ought to be passed over unread, and His Majesty should be expressly informed that the Estates did not ask to see them.

This was unanimously approved.

The Nobility then elected 6 members (two from each Class) as their representatives on the investigating committee.

Ibid., xii, 111-12

XV The downfall of the Regents and the Council, 1680

The Diet met in 1680 under the impression of Karl XI's successful defence of the country. The policy of the Regents was discredited; the financial crisis produced by that policy, acute; the Council was already politically in eclipse. Soon after the Diet met, the Commission appointed in 1675 (**XIV**) presented its report, which reflected severely on the Regents' administration. The Nobility was encouraged, notably by Hans Wachtmeister, to believe that they might escape financial contributions in future, and ensure the state's payment of their salaries, if they pressed on the Reduction (**XXIX**), and exacted massive financial restitution from the ex-Regents (extract (*a*)). Wachtmeister led a new group of King's Friends, concerned to provide the resources for reorganization of the armed forces, and prepared to that end to concentrate power in the King's hands: by parliamentary violence, by delations to the King, they went far to terrorizing the Nobility (extract (*c*)); and against them such high-aristocratic constitutionalists as Per Sparre fought a losing battle. It soon appeared that the report of the Great Commission might be made the basis of a prosecution (extract (*b*)); and though the Estates in 1675 had not claimed more than the right to investigate, they now found themselves manoeuvred by Wachtmeister and his friends into being both prosecutors and judges (extracts (*c*), (*d*), (*e*)). The Regents tried to dilute their responsibility by involving the Council; but the anti-de la Gardie minority, which had protested against his foreign policy in 1671, now disclaimed all responsibility (extract (*f*)). But the Council itself was now under fire from the royalists. It represented the historic constitutional check on the prerogative; it had presumed to give unsolicited advice against proceeding with the Reduction. The opportunity of striking at it arose accidentally, from an irrelevant speech by Robert Lichton (extract (*f*)). Wachtmeister used the opening to extract from the Estates the Declaration of 10 December (extract (*g*)); which, in form a mere restatement of existing law in answer to a royal enquiry, in effect left the King uncontrolled and irresponsible. It was a constitutional revolution, the moment when absolutism begins; and it had been contrived so that it seemed to come, not from action by the King, but by the grant of the Estates.

(*a*)

Minutes of the Estate of Nobility, 6 October, 1680

Herr Hans Wachtmeister rose again to suggest that if the administration during H.M.'s minority were called to account, means might probably be found to avoid any financial contribution hereafter, or at least that it would be only a little one; since after so many years of peace the country can scarcely have failed to accumulate a handsome cash reserve. At any time they might discover the clue to the abuses and disorders which have marked the administration. And it was not only for the period of the minority that a reckoning should be required, but also for the later period after H.M. had taken over the government. . . .

At this point several members, especially *Ekeblad*, pointed out that the Council must be consulted before any decision could be taken.

Herr Per Sparre: We are all agreed that we must lend H.M. a hand to the best of our ability, but we must discuss it first with the Council. . . .

Governor Mårten Reutercrantz: We cannot agree to anything until we see where the money has gone, and until private persons present their accounts.

Herr Hans Wachtmeister remarked that the Great Commission must come forward and show what they had done. The Estates have always had to contribute; [before 1674] the country had had peace for many years. If the situation is looked into carefully, it seems probable that resources will be found. . . . The Great Commission will no doubt shed light on the whole system, and we shall be able to see the source of all disorder. If things go on as in the past, no contribution will make much odds: it might just as well be thrown into the sea; it makes no difference how much we give.

Herr Hans Mörner agreed.

The Marshal: This question arises as it were incidentally, but I take it that the position is that the King has put the situation before us, and now asks for help; and from this arises the question of obtaining information and a statement of accounts for the administration during the King's minority.

Herr Hans Mörner and others: Not only for that, but for afterwards too; and there must be enquiry into who benefited, and who bestowed the benefits.

Herr Hans Wachtmeister with some others thought that it was no good just investigating the minority, but that they ought to ask H.M. to allow the Estates to enquire into the operations of the Treasury, and how it managed H.M.'s finances for the whole period from 1672 up to the present.

The Marshal said that he had received no permission to say anything of the Great Commission; but if the Estate were to ask H.M. for information from it, the request would probably be granted. . . . To this the Classes, and especially the Second and Third, answered Ay, ay. But the First Class said: We are prepared to agree, on the understanding that H.M. gives some relief from the heavy burdens that lie upon the country. There was some murmuring at this, and a number of members replied: When we have had a look at what the Commission has been doing, we can then have a look at the burdens.

. . . .

The Marshal asked if the Estate would approve the idea of sending to the other Estates to invite them to come up to the House this afternoon for consultations, so that we might try to get the same kind of united front as there was in Uppsala [in 1675]. . . .

It was unanimously agreed to confer with the other Estates on these matters; and *The Marshal* accordingly instructed the Secretary to go to the Clergy and Burghers and ask them to come to the House after dinner.

Svenska ridderskaps och adels riksdagsprotokoll, xiii, 6 *seqq.*

(*b*)

Address of the Estates to H.M., regarding investigation of the Regency's administration, 13 October 1680

After reciting the circumstances leading to the appointment in 1675 of a Commission of the Estates to institute the enquiry, the Address goes on:

The Commission thereupon met; and we now learn, from the exhaustive report which was made to us (with Y.M.'s gracious permission), as well as from the carefully-prepared documentary evidence attached to that report, that the narrative handed over to Y.M. by the Regents was not in fact provided with the appendices to which it made reference: so that the Commission was compelled to cause other statistics to be compiled, which appear on the face of it . . . highly compromising to the Regents; so that it must almost seem that the miserable condition of the finances . . . is to be ascribed to the administration of the country during Y.M.'s minority. And though we should be unwilling to impute to Their Excellencies, by anticipation, any conduct which now or in the future might be the basis of a charge against them . . . yet the business is of such high importance that it will not suffer us, nor will our duty as loyal subjects allow us, to treat it as a matter of indifference, still less to pass it over in silence. . . . We therefore most humbly entreat that Y.M. may be pleased to examine the report prepared by the Commission, and to give effect to it as may be most expedient for the safety and welfare of the country; and by so doing to afford to Their Excellencies an opportunity of bringing forward whatever they may consider to be capable of serving to excuse them.

ibid., 259-60

(*c*)

Minutes of the Estate of Nobility, 13 October 1680

Herr Hans Wachtmeister proposed . . . that in order to get the business finished more expeditiously, *The Marshal* when delivering the Address [(*b*), above] to H.M. should verbally ask permission for the Estates to elect a tribunal with full powers to pronounce a judgment on the charges, within a definite time, so that the case might come to judgment, and the judgment be duly executed according to law, during the sitting of the present Diet.

This was felt to be a dubious proposal, since there had been no discussion of it with the other Estates, and *Herr Per Sparre*, in particular, said that though he had no desire to enter into the merits of *Herr Wachtmeister*'s suggestion, they should remember that the Address had been drawn up by a committee, had been communicated to the other Estates, and by them agreed upon; and it could not now be altered by the Nobility alone, nor anything be added to it. . . .

Governor Mauritz Posse agreed with *Herr Wachtmeister*, and the more so since in H.M.'s letter to the Commission he indicated in plain language that he wanted the case brought to judgment. . . . At this there was considerable noise and disorder in the Classes, so that *Governor Gabriel Kurck*, and others, demanded that *The Marshal* permit them to vote by ballot, according to the Ordinance.[1]

The Marshal ruled that the matter was not of such difficulty that voting by ballot was necessary. . . .

On this there was a good deal of argument in the Classes; and in particular some members moved the question how far the Estates were entitled to pronounce judgments, and whether this was not a question that touched the King's prerogative; but the question fell away without a division.

The Marshal once again demanded that the Classes give their opinions; whereupon he was asked from the Third Class to put the question again, since some members of the Class had become so involved in argument that one said it was one thing, one another.

The Marshal: The question is, that H.M. permit the case to come to judgment, that the Estates may choose the judges, and (since this point has not been made entirely clear in the Address) that it be communicated verbally to H.M. when we carry up the Address to him.

Herr Per Sparre said that on the contrary that was *not* the question; the question was whether to communicate about it with the other Estates. At this speech *Herr Hans Wachtmeister* lost his temper, so that they came to high words, *Herr Per Sparre* and others insisting that the other Estates must first be consulted. And as *Herr Hans Wachtmeister* continually interrupted *Herr Per Sparre*, that gentleman protested, saying that if he was not to be allowed to deliver his opinion he might as well withdraw; to which *Herr Hans Wachtmeister* retorted that he couldn't do better; and that anybody who did not wish to stay was free to clear out.

Herr Per Sparre replied: What sort of breeding is it that shows a man the door?

Herr Hans Wachtmeister retorted that he was not showing anybody the door, but if a man would not remain inside, he could go outside. . . . As both gentlemen were now growing pretty warm, *The Marshal* intervened, requesting that the Classes should declare their opinion, which accordingly was done. And it was resolved that this point about judgment could not either be inserted into the Address nor verbally communicated to H.M., but must first be discussed with other Estates.

[1] i.e. the *Riddarhusordning* of 1626, which established the House of the Nobility and regulated its procedures.

The Address was then taken up to the Castle.

After *The Marshal* and the Committee had returned to the House,

Lieutenant-Colonel Nöding came forward, and complained vehemently that there were those in the House who threatened members, using the King's name, and other names also, and who told them that if they did not speak in such and such a way they would have a black mark put against them by the King and *Wachtmeister*. And he demanded that the House take him into its protection, saying that he had said nothing to deserve being threatened with the King's displeasure, or anybody else's. *The Marshal* and others asked *Nöding* to name the member who had threatened him. Whereupon *Nöding* named *Customs-Supervisor Cronskiöld*, saying that he had threatened him while the Committee was up at the Castle. Thereupon *Cronskiöld* came forward to the table . . . and related how he had discussed the question of the judges whom the Estates were to appoint with various persons, and possibly also with *Nöding*; and as he perceived that they had not all understood the business aright, he might perhaps have said that anybody who speaks against the King's interest will be taken note of.

At this *Lieutenant-Colonel Ramsay* came forward, and related that although he heard only the end of the conversation between *Cronskiöld* and *Nöding*, and could not say anything of its beginning, he could at all events say that there was talk of 'being taken note of by the King', and that '*Herr Wachtmeister* should know of it'.

Cronskiöld thereupon alleged that *Nöding* came to him and made a scene, complaining that they had not their freedom of speech as noblemen, but that 'if anyone says anything that does not please *Herr Wachtmeister* you can't be sure where you are'. To this *Cronskiöld* had replied by asking *Nöding* what he had against *Wachtmeister*, and said that *Wachtmeister* ought to know of it. *Cronskiöld* also said that *Nöding* did ill by thus seeking to stir up dissension.

. . . .

This led to great uproar and much hard feeling against *Cronskiöld*, and here and there in the Classes there were shouts of 'Anyone who says we speak against the King's interest is a villain'; and in particular *Admiral Horn* came forward to the lower end of the table, saying 'I consider any man who says that we speak against the King's interest is a villain, and so is anyone who threatens us with the King's displeasure, or with being taken note of. We all mean as well by our King as the next man. Such scum should be heaved out of the window.'

. . . .

Herr Axel Wachtmeister: Those who stir up the Estate like this are obviously up to some game or other: we had better keep our eyes open.

Herr Mauritz Posse, Herr Hans Wachtmeister, Herr Hans Mörner, supported *Cronskiöld*, saying that he had spoken like an honest man; and *Herr Hans Wachtmeister* said that if *Herr Cronskiöld* had not said what he did say, he would have said it himself. . . .

Others shouted that he deserved to be thrown out of the House. . . .

Governor Mårten Reutercrantz thought that the House ought not just to let the matter drop, but that the Fiscal should institute legal proceedings.

Herr Hans Wachtmeister spoke passionately to *Nöding* and *Ramsay*, saying that he knew how to bide his time, and would take such a revenge that no proceedings would be required. . . .

15 October 1680

Governor Conrad Gyllenstierna rose to inform the House that he had been asked by *Lieutenant-Colonel Nöding* to explain to the House on his behalf that although he had spoken nothing unbecoming to a nobleman or a man of honour, and was prepared to stand by everything he had said; nevertheless, in order to avoid any further unpleasantness, he would be glad if the House would forget what had passed between himself and *Cronskiöld*. He was himself prepared to forget it, would say no more about it, and wished the whole affair to be consigned to oblivion. . . .

When *Herr Conrad Gyllenstierna* had finished his statement there was a good deal of dissatisfaction among members, and it was said that *Nöding* had not behaved well to the House by allowing the matter to drop. Others thought that as the affair concerned the whole Estate, *Nöding* was not entitled to surrender their rights, and action could still be taken against *Cronskiöld*. But as this was no more than a muttering in the First and Third Classes, and as there was no formal proposal or debate, nothing came of it.

Ibid., 25-35, 41

(*d*)

Minutes of the Estate of Nobility, 15 October 1680

The Marshal reminded the House of what had passed on the 13th concerning the Address delivered to the King by the Estates. . . . And *The Marshal* informed the House that . . . the King had been graciously pleased to approve their Address, and had observed that since the Estates has so unanimously begun the business at the Diet of Uppsala [in 1675], and since H.M. still gave them his full confidence, the Estates might themselves nominate certain persons to act as judges and decide the case. . . . *The Marshal* accordingly asked the Nobility for nominations. . . .

At this there was for a short while a dead silence, no one offering to speak.

At last *Herr Per Sparre* said: I think that we ought to reflect that in the Address we say that the Regents and Council should have an opportunity to offer explanations; and that they must be given the opportunity before there is any question of appointing judges: . . . in their Address the Estates do not ask that judgment be pronounced; they ask that the Council may have a chance to make their explanations; and if H.M. should not find those explanations satisfactory, then it is for him to appoint judges.

The Marshal: Although the Estates did say in their Address that the Council ought to explain themselves, his Majesty has nevertheless been pleased to order that the case be tried, and that the Estates nominate the judges. I doubt whether we may venture to modify the King's wishes. . . .

. . . .

Herr Anders Lilliehöök: But the Address says that they may give their explanations; and obviously an explanation must precede any judgment; and by all the rules of law they ought first to be charged. Even a bailiff enjoys the protection of the law: he is given one and often two chances to make his answer to any allegations, and only after that is he summoned to stand his trial. . . . He desired that H.M. be put in mind of this, before any judges were appointed.

. . . .

Herr Hans Wachtmeister: There are precedents for the Estates' judging between the King and the magnates.

Herr Lilliehöök once again demanded that these things be brought to the King's attention.

Herr Hans Wachtmeister: Anybody who tries so hard to stop the Estates appointing judges may well be considered suspect himself. . . .

After a confused debate the three Classes agreed to nominate six persons of each Class, from among whom the King might then make his choice of judges.

Ibid., 35 *seqq.*

(*e*)

Minutes of the Estate of Nobility, 9 November 1680

Governor Conrad Gyllenstierna then rose in his place, and begged to remind them that they had chosen certain persons to be judges, with full power to act, over those who had directed the government during H.M.'s minority. . . . The persons they had chosen now desired to have the Nobility's guarantee and assurance that they would be protected from any legal proceedings in the future. . . .

Herr Hans Wachtmeister: It is only reasonable for us to guarantee those who have been named as judges: we should also guarantee each other, so that we bind ourselves to stand together and accept common responsibility for what has now been done – for, after all, times can change.

. . . .

After considerable discussion it was finally decided that the Nobility should guarantee those members whom they had chosen as judges.

. . . .

Herr Conrad Gyllenstierna reminded the House that a prosecuting counsel would be required. And suggested Fägerstierna.

Herr Per Sparre objected that the Nobility could not be both judge and prosecutor.

Herr Conrad Gyllenstierna: It is the King's wish that the Nobility should nominate the prosecuting counsel. . . .

Some were of opinion that H.M. ought to choose the public prosecutor, since he was plaintiff in the case.

Herr Hans Wachtmeister: No, the King is not the plaintiff; the Diet is the plaintiff, and it must appear by its counsel. . . .

Herr Per Sparre maintained that it was contrary to law, and a violation of established procedure. . . .

Resolved: that the choice of counsel be referred to H.M.

Ibid., 132–5

(*f*)
Minutes of the Estate of Nobility, 6 December 1680

. . . .

[*The Marshal* reported attempts to serve a summons on the Regents, and also on the Council.] At the same time a summons was delivered to the Council, addressed jointly to the Council and the Regents; but this could neither be received nor opened, since there was no one in the Council who had been a member of the Regency, or responsible for government during the minority: all they had done was to give the Regents advice. And the summons could not be received for other reasons also: many of the Council had been absent abroad;. . . the Council of the Realm [they said] was an Estate of the Realm, and it is not possible to summons a whole Estate, but only those members of it who transgress: if a priest transgresses there can be no question of summonsing the whole Estate of Clergy to answer for it. And so with other Estates. . . .

Ibid., 213-14

In the meantime *Herr Lichton* entered the House, and after he had sat a little while and listened to the debate, and in particular had found out what the point was about the Form of Government [i.e. that the Council had no corporate responsibility, or any responsibility in common with the Regents] he rose and said: the Form of Government says that the Regency shall rule with the Council's counsel. The question then arises: if the King should happen to do anything *without* the Council's counsel, is his action thereby invalidated, and can the Estates upset what has been done? 'Gentlemen' (he said) 'this is something worth thinking of, and we ought to debate it. We have the example of the late King's Testament: did not the Estates upset it immediately after his death? – and this despite the fact that when he made it he was a King of full age and authority. The same could happen to the actions of the present King, if we do not discuss it in good time, and take precautions; and who the devil can feel himself secure, if Kings are to be subject to this kind of thing?'

As this speech was utterly unexpected, and had no connexion with the previous debate, it took members some time to get their bearings, and there followed a number of irrelevant and conflicting speeches. . . .

Whereupon *Herr Lichton* resumed: I think it is a serious matter. Look at what happened to the late King's Testament.

As he said this he left his place and went up to other members, and what he said to them I could not really catch, though it was mostly about the upsetting of the King's Testament. They tried to get him to grasp what the present motion was; and some, in particular, said that Sweden was a kingdom so constituted that the King did some things alone and some things together with the Estates: things that concern the government of the country according to the fundamental laws, or war and peace, the King does with the Estates; and the Testament was a thing of such importance that it must be approved by the Estates if it is to have the force of law. . . .

But *Herr Lichton* stuck to his opinion that it was not a good thing for the Estates to upset what the King had done; and that time would certainly reveal the bad consequences of it.

On this topic there followed a prolonged discussion; but so many opinions were expressed, and so much was by way of conversation, that I could collect no more of it.

Ibid., 222-3

(*g*)

His Majesty's gracious Approbation of the Declaration of the Estates of the Realm as touching certain matters. Given the 10th December, in the year 1680

We Karl by the Grace of God King of the Swedes, Goths and Wends [etc.]:

Know all men, that Whereas the Estates of the Realm, out of that laudable zeal for the welfare of Our Realm which they have always shown, have taken into consideration (among other of Our and the Realm's high concernments) and dutifully weighed certain matters of importance as touching the government of the Realm: to wit,

First and foremost: how far the Form of Government, with the Additions that have been made to it (which was designed as a model or instruction for the government during a minority) may now be reconsidered by Us, who are a King of full age;

Next, how far we are obliged to govern Our Kingdom with the Council's counsel:

So now they have at last determined upon this resolution and declaration: That after careful consideration they have found that it conduces to the security and strength of Ourselves and Our Posterity, now and in the future, and that Our prerogative and the advantage of the Kingdom indeed require, that all Forms of Government, together with any Additions that may be made to them, can no longer be considered as binding Us in any way, but that We ought to be free to alter the same at our discretion in such manner as may be pleasing to Us and in the best interests of Our Realm and of all Our subjects; so that we are not pledged to any Form of Government, but only to the Law and lawful Statutes of Sweden;

Next; that when We undertake to govern Our realm according to law, and with the counsel of the Council of the Realm, this can be interpreted only to mean, that all decisions in matters which it is Our pleasure to communicate to Our Council (esteeming such consultation to be for the welfare of the Kingdom) must entirely depend upon Our own good and just judgment. . . . And that accordingly We, as a King of full age, to whom God has granted Our hereditary kingdom, to rule according to law and lawful statutes, are responsible for Our actions to God alone. But on the other hand a government during a King's minority is bound to answer and account for its actions whenever the King shall require it.

The Estates of the Realm, moreover, recollecting with the greatest veneration and satisfaction how We, like all former Swedish Kings, have always graciously permitted Our faithful subjects to approach Our royal throne and there receive Our own gracious pronouncements upon their affairs, declare that the Estates of the Realm ought not to recognize any Mediator, which is a thing not usual in our country, and should therefore be utterly abolished (**VII**); and that consequently the functions and duties of the Council of the Realm ought to extend no further than is enjoined upon them explicitly, as the true men and subjects of the King, by the plain words of the Land Law. They therefore cannot be considered as a separate, fifth Estate of the Realm; but are to be regarded only as of the same Estate as the rest of the Nobility.

Wherefore, perceiving the loyal tenderness for Our rights and prerogative, and for the welfare of the Realm, which the Estates of the Realm evidence herein, We have not only received the memorial of the Estates with a gracious appreciation of their good dispositions, but have signified Our entire approbation of the same; and We do herewith approve it, commanding accordingly that what has in such manner by the Estates been determined and resolved, shall hereafter for all eternity be received and obeyed as law and lawful statute, it being in Our power, in conjunction with the Estates, to make new law and interpret the old.

A. A. von Stiernman, *Alla Riksdagars och Mötens Besluth*, ii, 1873-4

XVI The consolidation of absolutism, 1682

The Diet of 1682 consolidated the authority of the crown, and confirmed the subordination of the Diet. Karl XI's plans for reform of army-recruitment involved the surrender by the Estates of their right to grant or withhold a levy of troops. Their right to grant taxes did indeed remain; but extract (*b*) suggests that the King would no longer tolerate a refusal. As in 1680, he (or his advisers) exploited with formidable effect the tactic of seizing upon a parliamentary inadvertence in order to manoeuvre the Diet into far-reaching constitutional concessions. The King's initial reaction to Anders Lilliehöök's not unreasonable speech (extract (*a*)) was perhaps nothing more than an outburst of temper by a monarch unduly sensitive about his royal dignity; but it was pursued so relentlessly that the Lilliehöök affair ended with the virtual abdication by the Estates of their monopoly of legislation, and the delivery of the law-making power, with only an insignificant reservation, into the King's hands. Freedom of speech in parliament, already menaced in 1680 by the activities of Wachtmeister and his *chœur de musique*, was now at an end: it remained only to extend its denial from the present to the past (**XVII**(*a*)).

(*a*)

Minutes of the Estate of Nobility, 4 November 1682

The second clause was read, of the project of the three upper Estates concerning the liquidation of the crown's debts.

Then *Herr Anders Lilliehöök* asked whether the regulations which were applied in the work of liquidation had previously been communicated to the Estates, since they were now treated as though they were law.

To which it was answered that such regulations were of long standing, having been made in the time of the Regency, and subsequently confirmed by His Majesty. . . .

Herr Lovisin: These are old rules; they have been in existence for over twenty years, and ever since they have provided the model for liquidation procedure. Many people have been dealt with in the past under these rules, and the rest ought to be dealt with in the same way.

Herr Lilliehöök: God preserve us from a precedent of that kind! If a thing is to be law, it ought to be agreed by the Estates; otherwise it isn't a law at all.

Svenska ridderskaps och adels riksdagsprotokoll, xiv, 49 *seqq.*

6 November 1682

The Marshal: I hope that what I am now to bring to your notice will be debated in an orderly fashion, and treated as confidential. I have this moment come from H.M.; and H.M. said that he had learned that some remarks had been made in this House about the regulations applied by the Liquidation Commission. . . . H.M. thinks that they may constitute an infringement of his prerogative, and accordingly asks for the relevant extract from our minutes.

Count Oxenstierna and *Ulf Bonde* thought it was deplorable that what was spoken and debated in the House should be reported and disclosed in this way. It would be best to send for *Herr Anders Lilliehöök*, who was clearly the person referred to. . . .

At this moment *Herr Anders Lilliehöök* entered the House.

The Marshal: I have just mentioned that the King sent for me and told me that he had heard that you had made certain remarks about the liquidation regulations, which H.M. finds to be an infringement of his sovereign rights.

Herr Anders Lilliehöök: I think it is quite deplorable that, in return for the honest services I have rendered, I should be traduced to the King, for a quite innocent remark, and traduced so foully as to provoke H.M. to anger, and lead him to ask for the official report of what I said. I thank God that I know what I'm saying, and the grounds for saying it; and I presume therefore that H.M. will withdraw his displeasure, and give due punishment to those who run about with such stories. I am a member of this House, and I consider that as such I am at liberty – this being a free Diet – to state my views and give any information I may have at my disposal. I know that there are regulations; but as they are nowhere clearly laid down, I do not know whether they are made by H.M. or by the Commission; and I want to know it. If they are, or are henceforward to be, considered as law, then I *must* know them. If they are on all fours with a contract, then it is only reasonable that those whom they concern should be in a position to know them, for otherwise nobody will know on what basis any agreement is founded. When the kings of Sweden make a contract with anyone they would not consider it legal or reasonable to act otherwise. . . .

The extract from the minutes was read.

Herr Lilliehöök: I want to explain that I don't feel that I have infringed the King's sovereignty: God forbid! I find that it says in the Diet's Resolution of 1680 that they [the Commission] shall be set up . . . but it says nothing of the regulations which have already been drawn up, and which we are now told are ancient; it speaks only of those which are to be laid down according to the Diet's Resolution. If I spoke in conformity with the law, I cannot have spoken amiss; and the law says that no one shall be deprived of his property save by law and lawful doom. And this must be done in the forms which the law prescribes; and the law by which a man is judged must be accepted by the Estates, and be put in force with their consent; and how can they have agreed to something they haven't seen? . . .

Ibid., 52 *seqq.*

7 November 1682

The Marshal: As I have it particularly in command from H.M. to say something concerning *Governor Herr Lilliehöök*, perhaps he would be good enough to withdraw.

Which he did.

The Marshal: H.M. has seen with particular displeasure the remarks of *Herr Lilliehöök* concerning the regulations for liquidation; and considers them as an impertinence and an attack on his sovereign prerogative, as tending to cast doubts upon those regulations which for long have been the basis of the Commission's proceedings. . . .

It appears to H.M. curious that *Herr Lilliehöök* should have wished at this stage to cast doubt upon regulations made more than twenty years ago, and subsequently approved and complied with by H.M. H.M. considers this as being a deliberate attempt to criticize H.M.'s conduct and to prescribe to him what instructions he is to give to his servants for the execution of their commissions. H.M. has therefore commanded me to enquire the opinions of the Estate of Nobility upon certain specific points which H.M. has caused to be drawn up: . . .

1. If *Lilliehöök* spoke with them about this beforehand, or if they asked him to speak; and whether they approve of what he said?

2. H.M. wishes to know whether those of the Nobility who have made loans to the crown, or are otherwise its creditors, have asked *Herr Lilliehöök* to put in a word for them and their interests; or if any of them has complained to him of having suffered any injustice.

3. H.M. would be glad to know what view the House took of his remarks. . . .

4. If the Nobility considers that *Anders Lilliehöök*, or anybody else, is entitled to draw up regulations for the liquidation, or correct or criticize the regulations already in existence?

5. If the Nobility consider that *Anders Lilliehöök*, or anybody else, is entitled to demand that the Estates of Nobility shall afterwards debate what the King has already done and sanctioned, or if anybody is of opinion that the King's hands should be so tied that he is not able, in his own dominions, to make laws, statutes, regulations and ordinances, and that the same have not the force of law except the Estates consent to them?

6. Whether it becomes a loyal subject with impudent words to limit the royal authority, or (as it were) to weigh the prerogative of his sovereign in a balance, when that authority is employed to the honour of God's name and the advantage of the realm?

7. Whether *Anders Lilliehöök*, or anybody else, is empowered . . . to determine how law shall be made and accepted in this country, and in consequence either to mislead others with otiose observations, or by untimely censures annoy H.M.?

Ibid., 63, 228-9

To these angry enquiries the Nobility, who seem to have been taken aback by this quite unforeseen outburst of royal ill-temper, returned a circumstantial answer, couched in language of fawning humility. They entirely dissociated themselves from Lilliehöök, repudiated his statements in the amplest manner, and in §5 of their reply went a long step towards abdicating the constitutional right of the Diet to control legislation: it is printed in the following extract.

5. In regard to the making of laws, statutes, regulations and ordinances within the realm, the Estate of Nobility are well aware that this is a matter which is competent to Your Majesty, as its lawful, Christian and proper sovereign, and they consider it as quite absurd to wish to force Y.M. to take the opinion of your Estates whenever you desire to make any statute, proclamation, regulation, or ordinance, or when Y.M. may find it necessary to issue instructions to any College or private person, or to inform them as to how they are to discharge the duties laid upon them, since all these things conduce to that obedience to orders which it becomes them to observe. . . . But such things are not to be esteemed or called general laws in the same sense as the Law of Sweden, which applies equally to the whole country, and to all Estates; and should Y.M. find anything in *that* law which it may be necessary to alter, or clarify, or improve . . . then it is accepted that the King has the right and the power to do it, and to appoint upright men, learned in the law, to supervise the business, which is then most humbly submitted to Y.M.'s gracious judgment and approbation;

and in such cases Y.M.'s faithful subjects of the Estate of Nobility presume to hope that Y.M. of your royal grace will be pleased to communicate the matter to your Estates, since it concerns them all in common: not that the Estates may or ought to prescribe to Y.M. in such things, but rather that – depending upon Y.M.'s gracious pleasure, and at such time as may seem best to you – they may thus have an opportunity (if Y.M. pleases) to put forward, in all submission, their humble thoughts, as loyal subjects, and this without any presumption or the slightest trenching on your Majesty's rights and prerogative, which the Nobility, as true and faithful subjects, are not less willing than bound to defend, to the utmost of their ability and to the last drop of their blood.

Ibid., 231

(*b*)

11 December 1682

The Marshal [reporting on the King's financial requirements]: Next, H.M. showed a plan for the fleet, at a cost of 4 *tunnor* of gold, which the Secret Committee had often looked at, though without coming to a decision upon it. H.M. therefore sent for some persons from each Estate, and showed us that 2 *tunnor* would not be sufficient. . . . There is a deficiency on the ordinary budget of 4 *tunnor*. The country is deeply indebted to the Bank, and to private persons. Credit is poor or non-existent. H.M. said that the Estates would not be allowed to go home until they produced the required amount, no matter where they take it from. The King has made up his mind; and the necessity is great. . . .

Ibid., 134

XVII The culmination of absolutism, 1689–93

By 1689 the theory and practice of absolutism had made such progress that the Diet and the Council (now the *King's* Council, no longer the Council of the Realm) could present the extraordinary document printed as extract (*a*), which imposes a retrospective censorship on parliamentary and administrative documents extending as far back as 1633. Four years later the Diet seemed to have reached its nadir of impotent subservience. The Resolution of that Diet (extract (*b*)) includes, in its §IV, the most famous, and the most ample, definition of Swedish absolutism: it is characteristic that it appears incidentally, almost as a matter of course, in a subordinate clause. But the Resolution reflects more than mere servility. It expresses the real gratitude of the nation for benefits which were really solid: peace, a balanced budget, order. These feelings appear still more clearly in the Reply of the Secret Committee (extract (*c*)) to the Secret Proposition of 4 November. That Proposition is indeed the climax of Karl's reign: an account of his stewardship of which he was entitled to be proud. It opens with a virtual acknowledgment that the Estates are entitled to know how the money has been spent which they have voted; it proceeds to a lengthy progress-report on every aspect of the work of the state. For the first time since 1560 a Swedish king can boast that he can 'live of his own'. The Proposition may in some respects flatter its author; but it reveals a really impressive achievement. Absolutism seems to have justified itself: after ten years of austerity, better times are in sight.

(*a*)

Act presented by the King's Council, together with all the Estates, for the cassation of sundry recorded minutes, discourses and speeches, containing improper matter concerning the royal powers, rights and authority. Given at Stockholm, 14 March 1689

We the undersigned, being the King's Council and the Estates assembled here in Stockholm for a general Diet, make known: that at this our assembly there were laid before us portions of the minutes of former meetings of the Council, from which we have gathered, by many particulars, that both in times of the sovereign's minority, as also in his absence, language has on various occasions been held of a most offensive nature, prejudicial to the King's rights, to his high authority, and to the good government of the kingdom. The passages are objectionable principally on the following grounds:

first, by the assertion that the King has no power to select his Council, or appoint to offices, or to rule and govern his realm, save with his Council's counsel;

secondly, that the King is bound to take an oath to adhere to the so-called Form of Government. And in this connexion the very grave and quite indefensible expression was used, that the King ought to have no voice in the Council, nor his coronation be permitted, until he has sworn to this same Form of Government;

thirdly, that the King's right and power to make and interpret laws is strictly limited;

fourthly, even though all the Estates had agreed on matters of national interest, and their decision had been approved by the King, a section of the Council at one time attempted to assert a right to utter their opinions, whether consulted and called upon for advice by His Majesty, or not; as happened in particular at the Diet of 1680, in the matter of the Reduction, and of the Estates' declaration concerning the royal authority and the office of the King's Council; and thus

fifthly, that the King's Council have been described as Mediators between King and Estates, and, indeed, as an Estate on their own account. . . .

It is with profound affliction that we find ourselves bound to conclude, from these passages, that some of Your Majesty's Council at that time had grown to such a height of ignorance or arrogance that they permitted themselves such abominations, and such baseless and indefensible remarks upon those high rights and prerogatives which so clearly and undeniably pertain and belong to Y.M., as hereditary sovereign of these realms. We have with all our hearts deplored, as we do now to Y.M. deplore, that such absurdities and impudent crazy opinions should have entered the head of any persons, and much more (and this we find especially distressing) of any members of the Council, and that they should not have shrunk from holding such language at the council-board, and suffering it to be inserted in their minutes; though it was in conflict with the fundamental law of the realm, with the King's rights, and with all preceding examples and decisions. From the humble duty and obligation which binds us until death to our most gracious sovereign, from the faithful zeal and unfeigned devotion which we bear to Y.M.'s high person, as our gracious, good, and incomparable King and master, we derive a deep horror and loathing for all such insubordinate speeches and discourses, and from our heart we wish that they had never been thought or uttered. And we find that H.M. has good cause to be in the highest degree angry with those who spoke in this fashion, and that he might justly prosecute and arraign them for such things. But since H.M. . . . daily shows that he tempers justice with mercy . . . we make bold, with the profoundest submission, and with hearts full of sincere devotion, to entreat that H.M. may be pleased to permit his wrath to be turned aside, and to order that all such offensive passages in the Minutes be abolished and annihilated, and that H.M., of his inborn clemency and of his mere grace, will consent that all such offences, now and for all future time, be considered as buried and forgotten. . . .

Stiernman, iii, 2056-7

(*b*)

Resolution of the Diet. Stockholm, 20 November 1693

[after some preamble] . . . Our most gracious King having been pleased graciously to look upon us, his faithful subjects and Estates, and for various weighty reasons to summon us and call us together; We therefore, acknowledging with the greatest reverence, and with thankful hearts, this instance of his royal condescension, in testimony of our punctual obedience have come together (as our duty is) in response to his most gracious summons; we have heard and received H.M.'s most gracious Proposition with all proper humility; and after due deliberation, as true and faithful subjects, we have thus unanimously agreed, resolved and concluded, as follows:

I

[Condolences on the death of Queen Ulrica Eleonora]

II

[Acquiescence in, and endorsement of, the revised provisions for a regency made necessary by that event]

III

Further, we call to mind the happiness that we still enjoy, in the preservation of the blessed state of peace, at a time when so many other kingdoms and lands are involved in a perilous war, and must suffer all the bloodshed and other miseries that war brings in its train. And since we can ascribe this happy state of affairs (under God) only to H.M., whose pacific temper and love of his subjects have always ruled and guided his counsels, to the end that the inestimable benefit of peace might not only be preserved to this realm, but also restored to the whole of Christendom; therefore our duty requires that with all humble reverence we do acknowledge the same. And we give to H.M. our most humble thanks that he has been graciously pleased to vouchsafe to his faithful subjects and Estates, through the Committee appointed for that purpose, an explanation and description of the state of our foreign affairs; desiring that God the Almighty may continue to bless H.M.'s counsels and designs!

IV

In which connexion we are bound to declare our gratitude to H.M. for his extraordinary condescension, as shown by the fact that although by God, Nature, and his high hereditary right (as well as by the humble declarations of the Estates . . . in answer to his questions regarding his absolute power) he and all his heirs . . . have been set to rule over us as absolute sovereign Kings, whose will is binding upon us all, and who are responsible for their actions to no man on earth, but have power and authority to govern and rule their realm, as Christian Kings, at their own pleasure; yet none the less it has been H.M.'s will graciously to inform us, by communicating to us the Secret Proposition regarding domestic affairs, of the most important matters that concern the stablishment of his royal throne and the happiness and welfare of us all. Whence we draw (in all humility) the comfortable tidings of Y.M.'s singular care, as a god-fearing and righteous King, to make sundry gracious ordinances, both for the fostering of piety and our pure evangelical religion, as also for the swift and impartial administration of justice; which are the twin pillars whereon all civil governments must rest their strength and security. Next, we learn likewise how H.M. has with the particular blessing of God continued the work, which was begun just after the last war, of reforming the recruiting of regiments, and maintaining them in good order; so that the Horse and Foot Militia (which have never been so formidable and considerable as they now are) have been so far put on the new footing, that when the little that remains to be done is accomplished, there can be no doubt of the success of the scheme; the Navy too having been strengthened with many ships of war, and by efficient and trained seamen.

As regards the work of the Commissioners for the Reduction, and for the liquidation of reduced estates, though their activities have been multifarious and beset with difficulties, we learn that by the laudable zeal and industry of those appointed by H.M. matters are now arrived at a point when the end of their task is in sight. Besides this, trade and commerce, navigation, manufactures, and all other means of livelihood of H.M.'s faithful subjects have been in the highest degree fostered and improved; whereby the revenues and resources of the realm have been notably strengthened and increased (and indeed continue to increase daily), the great debt is paid off, and all things brought into a good posture. And as we discern in this the evidence of H.M.'s care and pains for the advancement and welfare of his faithful subjects, so for our part we testify once more to our humble devotion, and to our thankfulness for his efforts. . . . And since the whole administration is now established upon a just and solid ground; and since the welfare of the realm depends (next the help of Almighty God) only upon preserving it in its present condition; therefore we undertake, one and all, as well for ourselves personally as for our constituents and our successors, that we will and shall hold unshakably to all that which has been so graciously established and well ordered by H.M.; and never, either directly or indirectly, demand or permit any alteration in it, but abide by it and defend it, as faithful subjects, though it be at the cost of our lives.

V

Lastly, we acknowledge with the deepest reverence the great boon which H.M. has been pleased to announce to us, that he will not on this occasion ask of us either any grant of taxes, nor any aid towards the expense of building royal castles and palaces, nor any aid for burying the Queen (though this has always been customary in the past).... This is a grace which we receive in all humility and thankfulness; and in return we bind ourselves to be ready to sacrifice our blood, our lives and all that we have, for H.M. and the heirs of his body, and likewise undertake that, if God should afflict this country with war, we will and shall not only punctually pay such contingent war-grants as were promised by us in the years 1686 and 1689, but also if the aforesaid contingent grants should actually be levied, and should prove inadequate to the needs of war, will remit it to H.M. to negotiate each year, for the duration of the war, for the raising of as large a loan as the necessity of the case may demand; which we collectively undertake to repay so soon as God shall give us peace again....

Stiernman, iii, 2094-100

(*c*)

From the Reply of the Secret Committee to the King's Secret Proposition. Stockholm, 13 November 1693

... What pains, toil and trouble H.M. has endured, and how many weary hours he has undergone in order to compass all that has been reported to us concerning the institution of the militia, the continuance of the Reduction, and the paying-off of the heavy burden of the national debt – of this we can form a fair idea; but we feel ourselves utterly incapable of finding words adequate to express our humble thanks to H.M. in a style suitable to our duty. This has been a work which few can appreciate, and which to many had seemed impossible: and it is, indeed, incredible that a single lifetime should suffice to its achievement. But as God's hand has always been over H.M., so even here He has made the task seem light, has strengthened H.M.'s energies, has forwarded the work, and has blessed H.M.'s efforts; so that we may now live in the happiness of knowing that the country's budget is balanced and its finances strong, that the huge debt which was so utterly crushing is now for the most part paid off, that the frontiers of the realm are so powerfully fortified that the welfare of the whole nation is advanced thereby. And as the whole system of government is now so fixed upon a firm and just foundation; and as the safety and welfare of the realm (under God) depends now only on all this remaining undisturbed; therefore we pledge ourselves, jointly and severally, to hold inviolably to all that which H.M. so graciously and wisely has established and appointed; and never, either directly or indirectly, to demand or permit any alteration therein, but like faithful subjects to hold to it and defend it with our life and blood.

Svenska ridderskaps och adels riksdagsprotokoll, xvi, 137-8

XVIII Some *dicta* of Karl XI

Karl XI was deeply conscious of his responsibilities: towards his people, and towards God. His absolutism was intended to be, and on the whole was, an absolutism within the law, as the mediaeval Land Law was now interpreted by himself and his advisers. He was completely self-sacrificing; his sense of duty was overwhelming. His intelligence was too limited for him to be able to formulate a coherent theory of kingship, and he was in any case too inarticulate to give expression to it; but in his intimate correspondence with his friend Nils Bielke his attitude to his job does from time to time emerge: the following extracts give some samples of it.

(i)

I desire nothing more in this life than to make a good end when the time comes for me to quit this painful world; for all that we do here is but vanity. And for this I daily pray to God, beseeching Him that the kingdom which it has pleased Him to commit to my charge may by His aid to be brought to such a condition that my successors and my faithful subjects may find in it their welfare and security. (To Nils Bielke, 13 June 1687.)

Karl XI:s bref till Nils Bielke, p. 24

(ii)

I wish that my income would suffer me to pay my ministers the same salaries as other potentates give to theirs. The spirit is willing, but the resources are weak; yet I yield to no one in the love I bear to my honest and faithful servants. If my service does not make them holy, at least there is no danger of its making them rich. (To Nils Bielke, 29 November 1687.)

Ibid., p. 33

(iii)

I have determined that I will never give anybody a title of nobility; for by the multiplicity of titles mere service comes to be despised. (To Nils Bielke, 7 May 1689.)

Ibid., p. 61

(iv)

As to the government's [of Pomerania] excuse that they have sworn to look to the welfare and preservation of their country, I should be glad to be informed by them whether my interests and the country's interests be not one and the same, and not two different things? For I ask no more of them than that they should keep such a militia on foot as may be sufficient to the defence of their country. (To Nils Bielke, 23 November 1689.)

Ibid., p. 67

(v)

It is best that I keep my hands free, and so arrange things that no one is accepted as mediator [between the participants in the War of the League of Augsburg] but myself. And when that moment comes, if the belligerent gentlemen won't have a peace, then they may fight away till they are sick of it for all I care, provided I don't have to send help in ships or troops. . . . (To Nils Bielke, 29 January 1691.)

Ibid., p. 84

B

THE SOCIAL CRISIS

XIX Resolution of the Diet of Norrköping, 1604

By a provision of Magnus Eriksson's Land Law (ca. 1350), it was laid down that the King was bound not to 'diminish the realm': should he do so, his successor was entitled to recover what had been alienated, 'if he can'. The alienation of crown lands and revenues by donations (as against their temporary alienation in the guise of revenue-assignments by way of wages, for instance) had grown appreciably in the last decades of the sixteenth century. This clause in the Resolution of Norrköping was designed to protect the King's right of recovery, to safeguard the legality of alienations *vis-à-vis* the Land Law, and by introducing a strictly conditional tenure to establish a kind of quasi-feudal relationship, alien to Swedish custom, between King and Nobility. The clause was to be of great importance in the subsequent history of the Reduction.

In the fourteenth place: We have also granted and resolved, that henceforward the Kings of the realm shall make no donations, or gifts of land or estates, except upon the condition that upon every change in the person of the sovereign, he who received such estates shall seek confirmation of them from the King who has succeeded to the government. Likewise that he be debarred from selling or mortgaging such estates, unless he has first made offer of them to the King from whom they were obtained. And if it should happen that he who gets such estates should die without male heirs, then the lands are to revert to the crown, and not to pass to collateral heirs. Provided however that if the recipient of the donation should leave a daughter, his sovereign shall be bound to provide her with an honourable dowry. And if it should happen that she takes as her husband such a man as is acceptable to the King, the donation may be continued to him, and to the lawful male heirs of their union.

A. A. von Stiernman, *Alla Riksdagars och Mötens Besluth*, i, 559–60

XX Alienation of crown revenues, 1612

The financial straits of the crown under the stress of simultaneous wars with Poland, Denmark and Russia drew attention to the fact that many of the crown-revenues were not available for military needs, since they had been temporarily alienated as *förläningar* – i.e. either as wages for civil servants or military commanders, or for the satisfaction of creditors, the reward of the deserving, or for other purposes; though the proclamation exaggerated in suggesting that 'virtually a majority' of all revenues had been lost in this way. The non-noble Estates at the Diet of 1612 demanded a Reduction – that is, the resumption of these revenues by the crown – as a means of avoiding additional tax-burdens. This was not quite the first time that such a demand was put forward, but henceforward it was to be repeated at intervals until 1680. Gustav Adolf did in fact resume *förläningar* on a considerable scale at the beginning of his reign.

Proclamation regarding the revocation of all revenues alienated during good pleasure, 26 November 1612

We Gustav Adolf etc. make known that whereas for sundry weighty reasons . . . we have been moved to summon the Estates to this Diet now appointed to be holden here in Stockholm, to deliberate concerning matters of consequence to this realm; and whereas now . . . it has been represented to our Council and Estates that they should take into consideration the means whereby this present great war . . . may be carried on, and the kingdom with its subjects be saved and defended from foreign occupation: So therefore it has been proposed (among other means) that we should revoke all grants of revenues [*förläningar*] which have been given anywhere in the country, and apply such revenues to the expenses of the war. And seeing that we do in truth find that virtually a majority of the crown's rents and revenues have been alienated in this way; and since few of those who have received such grants come forward to serve against the country's enemies, or do any other obvious service . . . we have therefore found it expedient to revoke all grants of revenues over the whole kingdom, Finland as well as Sweden, where such grants have been given during good pleasure, irrespective of the source from which they derive, the person of the grantee, or the authority alleged, and to place them all herewith in sequestration until such time as we are able to determine what grants every man has, and what service he does for them in return. But by this is not to be understood such farms and lands as have either by us, our late father, or by other of our predecessors, been donated in perpetual possession, and by us have been duly sanctioned and confirmed; but such gifts may be enjoyed and retained by every man upon the terms and conditions on which he received them. . . .

Svenska riksdagsakter, I Series, II, i, 243-4

XXI Gustav Adolf attempts to safeguard peasant rights, 1627

Though alienations of lands and revenues did not assume serious proportions under Gustav Adolf, the danger to the peasant's right of ownership was already appreciated, and it was in response to peasant complaints that the King promulgated this *Resolution and Declaration*. For the ineffectiveness of these safeguards in the next reign, see **XXIII**.

In the fourth place, there have been complaints that when we grant a man a farm or two in noble tenure as a reward for his services to us, or when we sell such farms for cash, it may happen that we may include the revenues from some freehold farms, and that in such cases the new owners lay hold on the rights of the freeholder, plague the peasant with unusual dues and obligations, and some of them even attempt to evict the freeholder from his farm and deprive him of his title. And since this is contrary to law and right, and we had not the smallest intention of infringing the well-established rights of anyone by such gifts or sales, we therefore declare that no one, whoever he may be . . . has the power to force any freeholder from his legal rights, or to burden him with new imposts, unless such imposts have been duly granted at a Diet. . . .

A. A. von Stiernman, *Alla riksdagars och Mötens Besluth*, i, 803

XXII Sale of crown lands, 1638

By 1638, military reverses in Germany, the ending of Swedish collection of tolls at the Prussian ports (by the Truce of Stuhmsdorf in 1635), and the cessation for the time being of payment of French subsidies, had made it impossible any longer to fight the German war mainly at the expense of the foreigner. The Regents were understandably nervous of increasing taxation. Despite the prohibition upon alienating crown lands during the minority, contained in the Form of Government of 1634 (**V**) they felt themselves to have no alternative. They took some care to safeguard themselves, and any possible purchasers; the amount they sold was moderate (equivalent to a revenue of something over 50,000 silver *daler* a year); but the term within which the crown was free to exercise its right of redemption was in 1644 fixed at far too short a period, and later inquisitions would reveal that purchasers sometimes obtained scandalously favourable terms, or even on occasion simply cheated on their bargains (see below, p. 114).

Minutes of the Council of the Realm, 1 June, 1638

The Council discusses how to raise money for the war.

Herr Matthias Soop: To mortgage or sell land to Swedes will not take us very far. If only we could bring in foreign merchants, from Holland or elsewhere, with whom we could bargain, then the price would go up.

Herr Clas Fleming: There is nothing to be expected here at home. . . . Little or nothing can be cut off the budget; a few persons might make some sacrifices, especially those who sit around this table; but the others live on their bare wages, as the hawk lives on his prey; and I don't see how it is practicable to cut down on staff. I don't like the idea of closing any of the Supreme Courts, or the schools etc.: we have just expanded the Supreme Court in Jönköping, and much it needed it. Perhaps the best means would be if we could find people who would lend at a reasonable rate: we might pay them 20 per cent, but in commodities and not in cash; or if need be we could mortgage crown land at 6 per cent. This would not involve any permanent loss to the crown, and it would be a measure which it would be possible to justify later.

The Chancellor [Axel Oxenstierna]: Selling at 3 per cent [i.e. at 33⅓ years' purchase] is better than borrowing or mortgaging at 6.

The Treasurer: I do not see how we can make a success of borrowing: we have borrowed before, and haven't paid; and we shall hardly get anybody to lend more. It is not feasible to impose any additional burdens on the country. Mortgaging will not give us enough. . . . Sale of land seems permissible; it will yield a good deal: suggested that we sell land worth 1000 *daler* a year. Adduced the following reasons for this:

1. the crown suffers no prejudice, since the income is safeguarded; 2. the land is better cultivated; 3. we have the example of the late King.

The Admiral: No King could reasonably annul something that has been decided by general consent, for the welfare of the country.

The Steward: When that time comes [i.e. when the Queen attains her majority] we shall have to produce our reasons, together with the state of the finances as they stand at present; and it will be obvious from that why we were impelled to use these very necessary means to save the fatherland from danger. It is the only resource open to us; we have no other, for it would be unwise to impose any further burdens on the country. We have done enough from our own resources, and made concessions of our own interests; and that must plead in our defence when the time comes.

The Marshal: We are forced to have recourse to these means by necessity; we are compelled to do what we would much rather not do . . . and I see no other means available; we must either borrow, or pawn, or sell. To anticipate next year's income knocks the bottom out of the finances. We must avail ourselves of this method; we must allot some provinces to anybody who is willing to put up the money . . . if we cut wages and salaries the yield will not be great; and the biggest cut will affect those of us who sit here round the table, and bear the burden; for the others no cut is really possible.

The Steward: . . . It might not be a bad idea to allot one particular province; but we must make a careful distinction between such provinces as can be spared, and those which have always been excepted by previous kings, and reserved for the crown, so that purchases are not made promiscuously.

The Chancellor: . . . The best way of all would be to develop the resources we already have; but in the meantime we are forced to use other means. Raising loans is usual and lawful all over the world. . . . Selling land is certainly a pretty questionable procedure as things are, and in view of the Form of Government; but there seems to be no other way out.

It was accordingly decided to have recourse to the means which had been proposed. If any King takes exception to this (though that is scarcely to be expected) it must be shown that we did it to save the country; and therefore we must provide against that event by inserting conditions and provisos. For if a King should refuse to confirm the sales, and should demand the return of the lands, it is reasonable that 1. They should be redeemed from the purchaser or mortgagee in good money.

2. If any purchaser has for his convenience incorporated such lands into his own hereditary estates or manors, so that they have become an integral part of them, he should be allowed to retain them, and to give the crown equivalent lands in exchange. . . . 3. He should get his interest back at 8 per cent per annum from the date of purchase. The King must therefore accept these conditions and provisos; for it he did not (which is not to be supposed) . . . and were to take back the land without restitution of capital, interest, and outlay on improvements, it would be a flagrant injustice; and this must be made clear to the King before he comes to the government of the country. . .

Svenska riksrådets protokoll, vii, 224-9

XXIII Peasant grievances, noble exactions, 1649

The author of the pamphlet from which this extract is taken was a good example of the rising official class: a parson's son who became tutor to a noble family, entered the royal service, had a successful career in diplomacy, and was in due course ennobled. His attitude to the social problem was probably influenced by his origin (the clergy very generally championed the peasants' cause) and by his concern as a royal servant for the rights of the crown: here the social and constitutional problems are seen to merge. The accusations against the nobility were certainly exaggerated, but they did have some substance; particularly before 1652, when the labour-services which could be required of former freehold peasants were limited by law.

There has for some time past been . . . sharp controversy about the rights of freehold peasants: a controversy which arises from the fact that for some years freehold revenues have been either given or sold by the crown to the nobility. This has produced a situation in which many of the purchasers have arrogated to themselves the same sort of authority over freehold peasants as they exercise over their own estates: indeed, they have imposed upon them heavier obligations than they lay upon their own peasants, and in excess of those which freeholders were formerly owing to the crown. First, by interminable *corvées*; then by many and unusual labour-services; thirdly by militia-levies, since the nobility (availing themselves of their privilege of designating who is to be conscripted) have passed over their own peasants and taken only freehold peasants, and this year after year. . . . With the result that the freehold peasant has been forced to accustom himself to accept the same conditions as the peasants of the nobility, or has been driven to surrender his property and his title to his noble landlord, who can then clap a rent upon the land as high as he pleases. . . . And to this end, indeed, some have allowed their freehold peasants to run up arrears on their obligations, and not only have refrained from demanding what is due to them, but have actually refused to accept it, so that when the three years were up[1] . . . the landlord would the more easily be able to acquire the ownership and title, and have some shadow of law on his side. . . . Those who have had the revenues of freehold peasants made over to them are inclined to argue that since the crown had the right to impose on the freeholder labour-services, *corvées* and week-work at its pleasure, so too the nobleman must have the same right, since the crown has sold or given it to him. They say: freehold peasants are of course bound to do building work on the crown's farms, fence its fields, maintain its parks, plough, sow, reap [etc.]. . . . And consequently they are now bound to do the same on the manors of the nobility; and should the nobleman abstain from exercising his rights over them, then they may reasonably be required to pay for the exemption, and buy themselves off for cash. . . . It is the view of some noblemen that the peasant ought not to be allowed too much liberty; for if he is not kept down he will get above himself, and then there will soon be no difference between a freehold peasant and a nobleman. If a peasant is to be any use you must keep his nose to the grindstone; and if the treatment is at first carried too far it can always be modified later, once the peasant has been broken to harness and learnt to respect the gentry. And what business has he at the Diet? Nowhere in the world have peasants as much liberty as in this country: the nobility can never feel safe from them. . . .

This kind of reasoning . . . is easily answered, the more so when it is shown to be not only bad morality but also bad law. For although an aristocratic constitution, or a mixture of monarchy and aristocracy, is neither unlawful nor condemnable in itself, yet here in Sweden it is so, since our constitution is, and always has been, of a different nature, and is not to be changed without the assent and approval of the King and of all the Estates of the realm. . . . The liberty which the Estates enjoy, of coming together at the Diet, and having their vote and voice there, is a liberty which is common to Clergy, Burghers and Peasants, as well as to the Estate of the Nobility. . . . And he who touches this liberty,

[1] A peasant who was three years in arrear with his taxes forfeited his farm to the crown.

touches the fundamentals of the constitution, and the law of the land. ... The question is not what the temper of the peasantry may be, or what sort of a person the common man in Sweden is by nature: the question is, what are his rights? The common man is always much of a muchness, whether he be Swede, Italian or Frenchman; and if the nobles happened to be peasants, they would be found to be of the same nature as everyone else. ... So that even if it were true that an aristocracy, or a monarchy mixed with aristocracy, would be an improvement on the constitution we now have (which however is by no means proved ...), it does not therefore follow that the constitution ought in fact to be altered; for no person, much less any Estate, will wittingly and willingly permit himself to be deprived of any of those liberties and rights to which he knows he is entitled – and has from time immemorial been entitled – by the law of the land. The King does not attempt it; ... and neither may the Nobility do it, for the one Estate has no power to exercise authority over another, and least of all to make judgments in its own cause, to its own advantage and the oppression of others. ... When from year to year, and from reign to reign, the privileges of the Nobility are increased, extended and improved, to the diminution of the royal revenues and the disadvantage of the other Estates; when one Estate is strengthened and exalted, and another is oppressed and trampled underfoot until at last it becomes an Estate no longer – then this is something which runs contrary to a monarchical constitution, and to the King's intention; it is contrary also to the liberties of all the Estates; and as it is repugnant to our law, and to the polity wherein we have now lived for many hundred years, we cannot suffer it, and it is a dangerous thing to attempt it.

Edvard Philipsson Ehrensteen, *Oförgripliga Bewis emot Adelens Rättighet öfwer Skatte-Gods* (1649), pp. 1-4, 26-29, 39-45

XXIV The Supplication of the Clergy, Burghers and Peasants concerning the recovery of crown lands. Delivered to Queen Christina at the Diet of 1650

The social crisis reached its climax at the Diet of 1650. The Clergy and the Burghers, who realized that the crown's alienation of revenues entailed higher indirect taxation, defied constitutional precedent by seizing the parliamentary initiative, and presented a solid front with the Peasants in demanding a Reduction. Queen Christina egged them on, in order to put pressure on the Nobility and induce them to acquiesce in her plan to have Karl Gustav accepted as Hereditary Prince: when the Nobility, alarmed by the attacks of the lower Estates, appealed to the crown for protection, and agreed to Karl Gustav's recognition, the Queen (having now got what she wanted) deserted her non-noble allies, whose only real gain was the statute of 1652, limiting extraordinary labour-services for freehold peasants whose dues and services had been alienated by the crown. But the lower Estates in 1650 did leave behind them this *Supplication*, a political testament which sums up, better than any other single document, the abuses of which they complained, and which exercised a continuing influence on the mind of the next generation, and was well-remembered in 1680.

As all the inhabitants of this country have great cause, at Your Majesty's approaching coronation, to offer heartfelt prayers that Almighty God may grant you His grace and blessing . . . : so We, the undersigned Estates of the Realm . . . have cause especially to represent to Your Majesty, in all humility, that during these last years of war the crown has been greatly weakened by the alienation of its lands, and its interests now require that those lands be restored to it in some convenient and proper fashion. For if this is not done, we cannot see how Your Majesty can maintain your royal state and authority, or how the government of the country . . . can retain its present shape and constitution. . . . And since we have no other object but to ensure that all things may go well for Your Majesty and the country (which we heartily desire), we beg that you may be pleased graciously to receive this our humble and loyal submission, not permitting any to put upon it a colour as though we should presume to prescribe to you what is to be done, and so to trespass upon your sovereign authority (from which God preserve us); for we esteem Your Majesty's royal power as the buttress of our liberties, the one being bound up in the other, and both standing or falling together. . . .

The first thing, therefore, of which we have to complain is that freehold and crown lands . . . have been alienated from the crown, and have passed in perpetual possession into the hands of certain Lords and private persons. . . .

Next, we learn with profound affliction that although by the blessing of God we have conquered sundry vast territories for the Swedish . . . crown yet Your Majesty from all this has little more gain than the mere names and titles of those conquered countries, but precious few of their lands and incomes: as though it had been for titles, and not for the good of the fatherland, that we strove and battled so long! Besides this, the good affection which we bear to Your Majesty and to our country is troubled because we see that instead of enjoying those fixed annual revenues which of right pertain to the crown, . . . Your Majesty is dependent on a parcel of uncertain and newly-devised imposts which are displeasing to the people, and cannot be collected without the impoverishment of the lower Estates and the destruction of the poor. . . .

It is also a lamentable fact that such extraordinary aids as are granted for a limited period, and for specific reasons, in order to carry on the war and surmount temporary difficulties . . . , not only tend to become permanent and perpetual, but are in part diverted into private hands; so that instead of helping us to bear the burden, . . . such persons make it the heavier, with the result that we are confronted with the prospect of taxes without end, and fall deeper into poverty year by year. . . .

The intention of the Estates of the Realm has never been that customs, excises, and other extraordinary war-aids should be regarded as the kind of impost from which the crown's certain and determinate revenue should arise: they were granted solely to give aid and support to the crown in crises, and at difficult moments of the war; and thereafter they were to cease, and every Estate was to revert to its normal fiscal obligations. But now we find that not only have they become the crown's sole and perpetual income . . . , but also a means for turning our liberty into a servitude, and of changing both the law and government of the country. All those who incite Your Majesty to sell land, or to give it away, must admit (for they make every effort to do it themselves) that it is better and safer for themselves and their children to put their money into land and fixed property, rather than to accumulate cash: why then should they say that what is best, most rational, and most profitable for them, is injurious to Your Majesty and the state? . . . Your Majesty is well aware what pains we have endured, and what tireless exertions we have made, during the present reign, in defence of our temporal and spiritual welfare against the greatest and most formidable foes; as also how many provinces we have (by God's blessing) won for this country and subjected to Your Majesty. . . . But what honour, what glory, has Your Majesty by the subjection of foreign lands, when some few only are allowed to possess them, and when on top of that they diminish the crown's ancient patrimony and property in the fatherland? Or what have we gained beyond the seas, if we lose our liberty at home? . . .

Churches, schools, *gymnasia*, hospitals, clergy, even poor sextons, have in many places lost their means of support when the crown lost its land. . . . The poor miserable widows of the clergy, to whom Your Majesty gave an undertaking that they should live tax-free on their little farms [for a year after their husband's death] have no benefit of your promise, but fall into a condition which is even more wretched than that of peasant widows, since they are not accustomed to day-work and servitude; the country's common soldiers, and especially those who are invalided, and have lost health and wealth in the defence of the fatherland, can scarce find a cottage-plot to live on, but henceforward will be forced to beg their bread. . . . Nowadays it is all but impossible for Your Majesty to make a journey anywhere in the kingdom, or stay in any town, without involving yourself in great difficulties and heavy cash outlay, since all the royal farms and manors are gone, which before afforded the King diversion and solace, and often gave him cause to tour the country, and at the same time inform himself of the condition of his subjects and listen to their complaints.

To sum up, then, unless remedial measures are taken, the whole constitution will be transformed. . . . From the many supplications, complaints and grievances which the commonalty daily bring forward, you will see into what an unheard-of state of servitude they have declined since private persons took hold of the country; for some treat their peasants ill, either by raising their dues, or by imposing intolerable burdens of day-work upon them, or by imprisonment, or threats, or evictions; until the poor peasant is totally ruined. And if any man should venture to complain of such usage, he will hardly find a court or a judge to take him seriously, unless he should go to Your Majesty and the Supreme Courts; and to these the commonalty can scarcely come, since for most of them they are too far distant; and even if they were not, the peasant would not risk it, on account of his simplicity, his poverty, and the snags which can crop up in such courts. And if he is so fortunate as to find an upright judge who gives a decision in his favour, the case usually peters out on the impossibility of getting a judgment executed, so that in the end the poor man must remain abandoned and shipwrecked. . . . Yet in spite of all this we find that there are nevertheless some who urge arguments on the opposite side. They say, for example, that under noble management the land would be better cultivated than was ever known before. Common sense and daily experience prove the contrary; for it is natural for a man to take better care of his own than of another's. . . .

If only Your Majesty would at your convenience . . . resume for the crown all freehold and crown lands, together with all territories won for this country during the last war; if you would restore the commonalty to its proper and normal liberty; if you would rule the country according to the law of the land, the Succession Pact, and King Gustav's Testament [1560] – then all this that we have mentioned could be corrected and amended; and since this is so, we beg Your Majesty to be pleased to consider these short points, . . . to the end that your government may be more firmly established, and our liberties receive protection.

1. That no land be sold or given in perpetuity, though meritorious persons may be granted land as a fief; and that every office may have a definite remuneration laid down for it, sufficient to support it, so that when a vacancy occurs and another is appointed to fill it he will be in a position to know exactly what his salary will be. . . .

2. . . . That Your Majesty may be pleased to order (and this we particularly request) that . . . each year revisory sessions be held in every circuit, when some of each Estate (under Your Majesty's presidency) may act as judges, and try all complaints of any infringement of the statutes of the realm, the rights of the crown, the liberties of the commonalty, and the coronation oath. . . .

4. No lands are to be sold, even if there should be a pressing need of money; but they may be mortgaged to inhabitants of the country, with the proviso that if it is a question of freehold land, the freeholder occupying it has a pre-emptive right to offer the crown a loan, and so acquire the rights of a mortgagee on his farm.

5. That no Estate may claim a monopoly of the service of the state, but every native Swede may by law participate therein, provided he is competent to discharge the duties of the post, and has been gifted by God with adequate intelligence, learning, discretion, and quickness.

. . . .

8. That all without distinction shall enjoy equality before the law. . . .

9. That the private prisons and torture with which some have racked and coerced their peasants, as though they were predial serfs, may be abolished, and stringently forbidden for the future, on pain of the severest penalties.

. . . .

It is to be wished that the good Lords and gentlemen [of the nobility] who are the present possessors and occupiers of the crown lands should amend their ways in these matters; bearing in mind that since it is contrary to law and statute that the lands of the crown be occupied by private persons, they have no prescriptive right on their side, and can hereafter claim no legal title of possession, now that the Estates of the Realm have called it in question....

And this is what we have found it necessary humbly to put you in mind of, in regard to this important matter....

Handlingar til Konung Carl XI:tes historia, x, 70-98

XXV Peasant grievances refuted, 1649-50

By October 1650 Christina had already made it clear that there would be no Reduction, and the aristocracy was beginning to breathe more easily. Their indignation at what they considered to be unfair attacks, unsupported by specific instances, is well expressed in extract (*a*) by Count Per Brahe (who was himself famous as an excellent landlord to his peasants), and by Axel Oxenstierna, who throughout his later life was insistent that the nobility could not afford to abuse their privileged position. Brahe's contention that the peasant could in fact obtain justice in the courts against tyrannical masters is, on the whole, supported by the evidence. Extract (*b*), though it begs some questions, makes a point of real importance.

(*a*)

Minutes of the Estate of Nobility, 15 October 1650

A joint committee of representatives of all four Estates meets the Council of the Realm to discuss the final draft of the Resolution of the Diet.

A peasant said: The nobility still go on buying crown land, which is then lost to the crown for ever.

Count Per [*Brahe*]: Are you suggesting that the sales be cancelled? Do you want the Queen to disavow her hand and seal and go back on her word? What sort of security would lawful acquisition give, if that were done? . . . could any honest man feel that his property was safe if we tried to get Her Majesty to recall her promises and break her pledged word? What would they say about her abroad in such a case? And whose fault would it be? If your trouble is that you grudge anything to anyone else, even though you are dealt with according to law and nobody does you any harm; if what you want is that we should all be at one another's throats; then think for a moment what our neighbours will say, and how they will utilize the situation! Is there anybody who is such an idiot that he does not see the consequences? If you look at it the right way, what is happening is really strengthening the crown: land which was deserted is now peopled and cultivated, for no one buys anything to his own hurt. And I may say that the Council of the Realm, for their part, had not expected to be told that they had not deserved well of their country: they have had troubles in plenty in these difficult years; and they made a handsome money contribution to the Danish war. And anyway, if you will consider the matter carefully, I can assure you that no more is now asked of you than was asked when you were under the crown; and you did not complain then, in spite of being oppressed by evil and unrighteous bailiffs. You talk about 'Livonian slavery'; but that's not fair. . . . Here you are treated well; you are a free people; . . . you can have your sons and daughters at home; you may place them where you will; you can move from your farm if you want to, and nobody can stop you. So take care what you are doing, and don't go stirring up dissension. . . .

A peasant said: We have no rights; they take from us all that we have. The aid which used to be called Ship-Money has now been pocketed by the nobility.

He was asked who was his lord, since he complained that he had been deprived of all that he had . . . ; but the peasant would not tell the name. But at last he said that it was Count Linnar [Torstensson]; but would not admit that the Count had dealt so with him; and later could not remember what it was he had said.

Count Per: We managed to convince you on a previous occasion when I talked to you; and we told you then the reason why the nobility had got possession of Ship-Money: it was in return for our surrender of exemption from customs-dues [in 1644]. . . . You may complain of your burdens as much as you like; but I tell you that you have never had it better than now. But I suppose that you will go on complaining until you are free of burdens altogether. . . . Clergy, Burghers and Peasants – they are all in clover these days; though just at the moment, perhaps, they may be suffering some hardship as a result of the unexpected scarcity which prevails this year.

The Archbishop [*Lenaeus*]*:* What they say is true, all the same; we know it, because whereas in former times there was a handsome income from tithes, they have now dropped very much. And I am afraid that there are more of those who treat the peasants badly than of those that help them. There are certainly grievances....

The Marshal of the Diet: You make sweeping charges, but you offer no proof. I have already told you that you should name those who oppress you, and then you would have justice: how can we reach a verdict if there is no defendant?

The Chancellor [*Axel Oxenstierna*]*:* You have a good deal to say about the number of taxes. That's as may be; but I could show you what revenues we have had ever since King Erik's time, and how far the money went. It did go some way, certainly; but in those days wars were not what they are now.... The German war was a very different affair from any that preceded it: it needed more men, more ammunition, higher pay; and how far would the old revenues have gone in such circumstances? The Ship Money you speak of is an aid dating from very ancient times;... but it is not suitable to times like these. It is an anxious business to devise other means for carrying on the government: the wars have largely been financed from the sale of lands[!]; but we should certainly not have needed to fall back on that expedient if we could have got hold of money.

The Peasant said: In Uppland there are hundreds of peasants who have passed into the hands of private buyers of land who certainly never did the crown any service, or brought it any benefit.

The Chancellor: Although the commonalty may not be able to see it, their services have in fact been of real use; and perhaps if they had not been available we should not still be at peace. During the last war with the Danes it was [Louis de Geer, against whom these complaints were directed] who got us ships from abroad and so gave us the upper hand; and but for that we should have had a Danish invasion....

The Archbishop: The Peasants have asked our assistance, and we can do no less than intercede for them. When we told them that they should name those who have done them wrong, they replied 'We are making general complaints, and we are not going to risk naming anyone in particular, for fear it will go harder with us.'

Count Per: And so all must pay the penalty, because you make a general accusation! What sort of law is that?

The Peasants: If we are going to bring an action, we'll bring it in the Supreme Court; but it takes more time than we can afford. One woman has been waiting here for over sixteen weeks.

Count Per: A man can't be in two places at once. Of course these things take time. And anyway the woman may not have been as much in the right as you think. But if you good men will bring a complaint, when you feel that you are suffering hardship, you shall have justice, and we'll let you see that we are serious about it: there was a case only the other day when someone was punished for oppressing the commonalty.

The members of the Council now rose, and asked the members of the Committee to refer to their respective Estates the explanations which had been offered. Whereupon the meeting broke up.

Sveriges ridderskaps och adels riksdagsprotokoll, iv, 424–31

(*b*)

An Aristocracy open to talent? (*1649*)

See the headnote to **X**.

Sir Peter [to *Master Hans* the parson]: I seem to remember that you made use of the expression that the nobility was too numerous, too great, too powerful, and so forth. But what do you mean by 'too numerous'? Have you reckoned up whether they are more numerous now than they used to be in the old days? Have you fixed a definite number which they are not to exceed? Have you intimated to Her Majesty just how many noblemen you are prepared to have in the country, and given her to understand that she must see to it that they increase no further? Well: it may perhaps be the case that they *are* too many, that there are more of them than there were twenty or thirty years ago: is that a cause for apprehension? is it anything to be afraid of? . . . Whence comes that increase which makes you complain that the nobility is too numerous? Whence indeed but from your own Estate! It is your own relatives, your sons and sons-in-law, who by their good services have so advanced themselves, that now they are added to the Estate of Nobility! Are they therefore to be accounted traitors who are trying to overturn the constitution, whose property is therefore to be taken away from them, and themselves made peasants once again? . . . You say that the nobility is become too great and powerful: in what, then, does that power consist, that causes you such alarm? To the best of my knowledge there is no castle or stronghold in noble hands. They have no private armies on foot, wherewith to make themselves formidable, nor means to raise any. They are not so absolute in their offices and their governorships that they are free to do as they list. There are many more princes in France than counts and barons in Sweden, and more noblemen than we have freeholders, and all with such resources and incomes as we cannot hope to match; yet this is accounted to be a source of strength and honour to that crown. Nobody there makes these things a matter of accusation against them, or clamours that their lands be taken from them, and the whole Estate be reduced to ruin. And if you are disposed to argue that the wealth, power and authority of the nobility is evident from the fact that in their dress, their domestic circumstances and other outward shows they conform to the customs of the world, and put themselves on a common footing with their social equals, – then you are deceived in that too. I concede that there are visible distinctions, and that our nobility, by way of showing their respect for Her Majesty, dress with the elegance that befits them, and put themselves to great expense by doing so; they do not willingly appear in patched garments if they can at all avoid it, nor do they pester their sovereign to give them money for new clothes when they come up to the Diet, as members of your Estate are used to do. But what then? Their wealth is certainly not increased thereby. I verily believe that our noble forefathers, who contrived to manage with a homespun doublet and glass buttons, and had small windows in their houses, and one or two servants whom they paid six marks a year, were better off than we are . . . !

. . . Another thing which seems to be a sore point with you is that the nobility is preferred to the rest of you for the important offices of state; which you conceive to be a slight and an injustice to you. But this I refuse to take seriously. I should be glad to know just which offices you suppose yourselves to be excluded from, to the nobility's advantage? You see yourselves from daily experience that any man of character and capacity who does the state good service can without difficulty enter the Estate of Nobility, whether he spring from clergy, burghers or peasantry; with the result that our nobility has so increased that some hundreds of new families have been founded. And once a man has gained entry to the peerage he has as much right to office, and finds it as easy to obtain it as anyone else . . . ; but that a man should at one bound jump from his pepper-bags or his dung-cart and put his filthy hands on the highest office – that is something which would never do. But in the meantime there are (nevertheless) many important and profitable positions for which your Estate can compete on an equal footing with the nobility, and sometimes, indeed, with an advantage over them; all army ranks from that of colonel downwards can be filled by men of your Estate just as well as by nobles; admirals and ships' officers may equally well be of non-noble as of noble birth; secretaries, treasury officials, customs officials, inspectors, burgomasters, the staffs of the chancery and the exchequer, bailiffs, accountants, magistrates – in sum, the whole personnel of the country's government – consists of the *plebs*, and to the best of my knowledge no one who is a nobleman born ever fills these posts. So too in the Supreme Courts one half of the judges are drawn from the non-noble Estates. Add to this the whole of the clergy, with their many wealthy sees and benefices – though in past ages such positions were almost always in noble hands. . . . If society were not ordered on lines such as these [i.e. with the reservations of the highest positions for the aristocracy] you would soon discover for yourselves that government could not be carried on. If you, *Parson Hans*, were to sit in the Chancery and deal with a mass of foreign correspondence concerning external affairs; or you, *Nils Andersson*, had to play the courtier and serve Her Majesty as Gentleman-in-Waiting; or you, *Jack*, were to sit on the bench in the Exchequer or the War Office – do you think that the government and the country would get much good of your services? . . . So I conclude that the best and wisest solution is that every man should stick to his Estate and his function, as in the past, lest it should happen to us as to Aesop's frog, who aspired to be bigger than she was, and burst in the attempt to make herself so.

Samtaal emellan Juncker Päär, Mäster Hans, Niels Andersson Borghare och Joen i Bergha Danneman, pp. 39–41, 51–3

XXVI Karl X Gustav's Reduction, 1655

By the time of Karl X Gustav's accession in 1654 it seemed to be obvious that some measure of Reduction could hardly be avoided. Alienations had now reached such a pitch that perhaps two-thirds of all the crown's land had passed out of the King's hands. In 1655 Karl Gustav presented the Council and the Nobility with an ultimatum: either they must make massive annual payments, or they must consent to a measure of Reduction. In the past two or three decades the Nobility had on successive occasions assented to increasingly serious infringements of their fundamental privilege of fiscal immunity: they now quite regularly paid what was virtually a tax, under the name of the 'contribution'. A Reduction would affect only those who had received donations from the crown; while the contribution bore heavily upon all, and dangerously weakened the whole concept of privilege. It was in the hope of recovering their traditional immunity that the Nobility, guided by Erik Oxenstierna (who had inherited his father's wariness of committing himself to untenable positions), decided in effect for a Reduction: its terms are printed below. The Council was able to resist a demand, strongly pressed by the lower aristocracy, for a graded scheme, which would have proportioned the fraction to be restored to the amount of crown revenues received: instead, they forced the acceptance of restitution at a flat rate of one-quarter of all donations received since 1632. It was an early indication of the differences in view and divergence of interest between the high aristocracy and the low. The Reduction statute, by hinting at distinctions between 'meritorious' and 'unmeritorious' recipients, and by providing for an inquisition into the sharp practice which on occasion had accompanied the acquisition of crown lands, paved the way for the terrible retribution exacted by Karl XI in the 1680s. The Reduction was entrusted to a commission, soon to be known as the Reduction College. It proceeded forthwith to reduce the so-called 'inalienable' lands; progress in reducing the quarter-part was held up by the King's long absence abroad. In the meantime former beneficiaries continued to pay the monetary equivalent specified in the statute. Hence in 1660 the Nobility themselves took the initiative in securing that the work of Reduction, in terms of the statute of 1655, was resumed – not least because they regarded that statute as a final settlement, guaranteeing undisturbed possession of the three quarter-parts which it left untouched. This had never been Karl Gustav's interpretation, nor that of the non-noble Estates, who looked forward to a continuing Reduction. Their view of the matter was to be emphatically confirmed, twenty years later, by Karl XI.

From the Resolution of the Diet of Stockholm, 1655

IV

The problem of how most conveniently to provide the resources required for the government and defence of the realm, while at the same time keeping taxation at a level tolerable to the King's subjects, has produced various proposals from a long succession of Diets; and at this present meeting seems more serious than ever. For it has been borne in upon us that if the King is not to find the conduct of the government altogether too heavy a burden, and if the country is to escape irreparable harm, it will not be enough to levy extraordinary taxes, but some speedy and permanent remedy must be found, which will provide the ordinary revenue with steady support....

In the first place we find it necessary that the landed estates of the crown be put in better order than at present. For although certain portions of them may for various reasons have been handed over to the inhabitants of this realm, with advantage to the yield of the soil, it is nevertheless obvious that abuses have crept in, which in many cases produce notable infringements of the rights of the crown, and notable damage to the revenues. And we are therefore very ready – despite the losses which we must in consequence sustain – to subordinate our private interests to the welfare of our fatherland. In particular, in so far as any of us may have a share in the landed estates which have passed out of the crown's hands in recent years, we are prepared, out of hearty good-will to the service of our King and country, to grant that a reasonable and moderate Reduction may be applied to them, though only within certain limits, which are set out below. But in order that from the very beginning the ambit within which this same Reduction is to operate may be plainly laid down, and in order that its effects may not reach too far back into past times . . . it has been agreed that in the investigations which are to follow, the sixth of November 1632 . . . shall be prescribed and laid down as an unalterable terminus, so that whatever land was sold, donated, or by any other lawful means conveyed away from the crown before that date, shall be fixed and undisturbed in its present ownership, . . . and shall in no wise be challenged, . . . either now or in the future. But on the other hand everything which has been alienated from the crown subsequent to that date is to be subject to the Resolution of this Diet, and the conditions laid down in it, and is to be rigorously scrutinized and examined, accordingly. We have also freely consented, in order to prevent mistakes, that everyone who after the aforesaid date, 6 November 1632, may have obtained land from the crown (whether freehold land or crown land) shall be bound to produce his title-deed to those whom His Majesty has undertaken to appoint for this purpose, and thereby substantiate upon what terms . . . he holds it. . . . If a man shall appear to have acquired land from the crown by purchase or exchange, but is proved on investigation not to have paid what was due for it, in money, money's worth, or other equivalent revenue, according to the official valuation at the time when the purchase or exchange was effected, then he may reasonably be called upon to indemnify the crown for the loss it has sustained. . . . This however is not to be construed as applying to cases where it is expressly stated, in the title given by the crown, that the sovereign by his grace and favour (and hence of set purpose, and in the exercise of his royal prerogative) has made grants in excess of what he received again by way of exchange. . . .

We have given particular attention to the question of what lands and revenues of the crown may have come into our hands in recent years. ... And in this connexion we have called to mind that certain places have for many years been reserved for the convenience of the sovereign, or for the maintenance of the army, the working of the mines, or other useful purpose, ... so that they have never [hitherto] been disposed of, or at least only with so sparing a hand that no great sense of loss was occasioned by it. For this reason, and because we are informed that of recent years many such localities and estates have been lost to the crown, and have become noble land either by purchase, mortgage, or by the crown's repayment of loans or acquittance of debts, and also through the favour and gracious inclination of the sovereign to reward good services; we have taken into consideration all the circumstances which seem to be involved, and now declare as follows: that ... all such places as may be considered absolutely inalienable should be roughly described and enumerated in terms of certain general criteria. ... We therefore suggest that ... among those places which are accounted to be inalienable land shall be reckoned all those enumerated in the following categories: [18 categories are enumerated]. ...

... And to show our most loyal devotion to His Majesty, and to the welfare of the country, we of the Nobility ... freely offer to His Majesty our most gracious King and Lord, to surrender and restore all the places and estates which may reasonably be understood as falling within the above descriptions, and which have passed from the crown into our possession since 6 November 1632, by whatever means, together with all the revenues and rights which we have acquired with them, ... on the understanding, however, that the procedure shall be modified according to the different circumstances in which each was acquired ... as follows: 1. That which was alienated from the crown purely and simply as a gift emanating from the King's benevolence shall be restored without any sort of *quid pro quo* or compensation, except where the property has been notably improved by the investment of capital; and this is to be assessed by impartial arbitrators drawn, as to a part of them, from the nobility, and the present owner reimbursed according to their award. 2. If any man has bought from the crown the right to the peasant's taxes on the estates which have been donated to him, he is to prove how much he paid, and to be repaid that sum, before he is forced to surrender his rights and his lands. 3. If land has been given by the crown as security against a loan, and the crown's indebtedness is established, he who advanced the money is to enjoy possession of his security until he is paid what he advanced; but he must restore it upon repayment. 4. If land has been acquired from the crown by purchase or exchange, or by way of settlement of genuine debts or advances, it is only reasonable that the purchaser, or he with whom the land was exchanged, be repaid (or receive appropriate compensation) before handing over the land; though proof must be offered of the circumstances of the sale or exchange, and they must have been in conformity with the law, and not have involved the obvious or demonstrable swindling of the crown . . . and payment must be calculated and proportioned accordingly. . . .

20. And as we of the Nobility will gladly do our utmost to ensure that the finances of the kingdom may be put on a sound footing, but are conscious that the recovery of the aforesaid inalienable lands is not in itself adequate to that end, we have in addition . . . most humbly offered to His Majesty, and herewith of our own free will do declare: That besides the inalienable lands, we will give back to the crown, in perpetual possession, one quarter of all such landed property, and of the rights and revenues appurtenant to it, as has been given and donated to private persons by the mere generosity of the crown since 6 November 1632. . . . Since this has now been consented to, we should have been most willing at once to hand over to His Majesty our quarter-part in the form of land; but since it is most necessary that there should be an investigation before it is clear what this implies, and since His Majesty's revenues in the meantime will continue to be uncertain, we have accordingly declared that we will make a money payment equal to the presumed revenue from the aforesaid quarter-part, according to the method of calculating the determinate and indeterminate revenues which is usually employed in the Exchequer, and according to the official tables of valuation. We will accordingly, for the next three years, hand over to His Majesty in cash one-quarter of all revenues donated to us since 6 November 1632, . . . and in the meantime every man is to present himself to the Audit Office, and there correctly specify which of his lands he would wish to be reckoned as his quarter-part.

A. A. von Stiernman, *Alla Riksdagars och Mötens Besluth*, ii, 1236–50

XXVII Social strains within the Nobility, 1660

In 1655 the authority and prestige of the Council had been sufficient to ensure

that the partial Reduction then agreed to should not be deliberately weighted against the high aristocracy. When the next crisis came, at the end of the 1670s, they were unable to repeat this achievement. It was not only that they had been discredited by their political record (**XIV**): it was also that they were now the objects of the envy and jealousy of their less fortunate colleagues in the Estate of Nobles. The grounds for this feeling, and the nature of the cleavage between high aristocracy and low, are revealed in the following excerpt from the debates on the Addition to the Form of Government (**XI**).
From the first version of the Observations offered by the Nobility upon the draft of the Addition to the Form of Government, Oct. 1660.

4. It is further the earnest request of all the Nobility that in the choice of persons for the Council of the Realm, as also in the appointment to other offices, both civil and military, no regard shall be paid to the Class to which the candidate may belong, but that the criteria for appointment shall be qualifications and meritorious service, so that persons may be selected according to their fitness for the post, and not posts adapted to suit persons. . . . *Item*, that those who hold an appointment be not removed from it without good reason and lawful sentence; and also that they be not denied promotion, if qualified to obtain it. And in particular we request that native-born Swedes of noble birth may be employed on state affairs in the Chancery, and in diplomatic posts; and that the Swedish regiments be furnished as far as possible with Swedish officers, though without prejudice to foreigners who may be qualified, and may already have a record of service in those units.

5. The Nobility take this occasion to observe, that for some time past the posts of Master-General of the Artillery, Master of the Horse, Master of the Hunt, President of a Supreme Court, Governor-General, General, Lord Chamberlain, Marshal of the Court, Colonel of the Guard, and Postmaster-General have been appropriated solely to members of the Council, though in former times they were filled almost always by members of the nobility who were not of the Council. They now request that these positions, like others in the civil and military service, may once more be open to them; and in particular that the rank of General (though not that of Field-Marshal) be restricted to those who are *not* of the Council, so that when anyone is called to the Council he must resign his position as General. It would indeed be for the public service if members of the Council were debarred from holding any other public appointment; and we urge that this rule be adopted and observed. Nor do we think that any nobleman ought to

hold more than two posts at the most, (and they should be not incompatible with one another) from which he draws a salary.

. . . .

9. Since it is plain that abuses have resulted from the naturalizing of foreign noblemen, it seems reasonable that the practice should be limited in the following ways: (1) that no one be naturalized, now or in the future, save with the advice, approval and knowledge of the Council of the Realm; (2) naturalization to confer no more than one vote in the Estate of Nobles; (3) such persons not to be admitted at once to the more important offices and positions.... And just as we consider it to be repugnant to the law that those who have been naturalized should at once be raised to the dignity of membership of the Council, so also we request that such membership should not in future (as it mostly has been, for some time past) be reserved to those of the First and Second Classes, but that it be drawn impartially from all three, in conformity with the express provisions of the law; and that in choosing members no attention should be paid to ties of blood or friendship, but only to loyalty, honour, intelligence, responsibility and good service.

10. To the end that every office may be secured in its honour and dignity, and also in order to avert misunderstandings between the Estates, it is requested that the Regency and the Council be pleased to draw up a Table of Ranks for the civil service, so that no one shall be able to usurp the precedence of another, as happens only too frequently but every position may be accorded its proper degree of dignity, and every man be placed in company according to his position on that scale, and not according to his seat in the House of Nobility; though care will be required to resolve the competitive claims of civil and military office....

Svenska ridderskaps och adels riksdagsprotokoll
viii, 193-5

XXVIII Gustav Bonde's political programme, 1661

In the Testament which Karl X Gustav had made upon his death-bed, he had designated Herman Fleming for the office of Treasurer during the coming minority. His purpose was to ensure the continuance of the Reduction, for of this Fleming had been one of the most zealous advocates. But for just this reason Fleming had made himself unpopular among the high nobility; and under their influence the Diet of 1660 did not hesitate to upset Karl Gustav's will in this particular, as in some others. Fleming was rejected; Gustav Bonde was chosen in his place. Bonde was a member of the inmost circle of the high aristocracy; but he was a highly intelligent conservative who realized that a moderate Reduction was necessary to save his Order from worse things, and was also gravely concerned at the growing social cleavage within the Estate, and at the serious constitutional consequences which might be the result of it. He therefore urged the old families to stop snubbing the newer peers, and to be more ready to accept the hierarchy of state service as a criterion of precedence. His remarks on the need for economy, and hence for a pacific foreign policy, reflect the clear-sighted, illusion-free sobriety of his assessment of his country's real position and requirements.

Memorial read to the Council of the Realm, 26 June 1661

[After a preamble],

If, then, I examine the reasons for our present condition – which appears to me as exhausted and feeble, in comparison with that of other countries – I find the sole cause to be the great lack of financial resources which afflicts this country; so that no matter what plans may be devised ... to strengthen it, their execution is invariably hampered by lack of means, so that every salutary measure is thwarted, and many advantageous schemes have to be abandoned. ... It is quite clear that all the servants of the state have such large arrears of salary that virtually all their private means remain in the hands of the crown; with the result that they suffer such privation that they can no longer do their work, and our provinces are left in a hazardous condition; and all this because the crown is impoverished. So that it seems that it would be well worth while – and is, indeed, imperatively necessary – that care should be taken without delay to see whether the state might not be brought to a condition in which it could live of its own resources, and not always be forced to seek help from others, and become their pensioner; but might be enabled by its own strength to show its teeth to other powers, if the need should arise. And this, as far as I can see, will never be possible until we discover the real causes of the poverty, both of the community and of the private individuals who comprise it, and then try as far as possible to remove these causes, and prevent them from recurring. And though no doubt the reasons are many, for the moment I suggest only two: first, the many exhausting wars which this country has had to bear in recent years; and secondly, the abuse of the country's direct and indirect revenues.

[After considering the first of these (**XLI**) he goes on:]

We must therefore eliminate the *second* cause of our poverty, which was defined as the misuse of the incomes of the crown. And this can best be effected by economy. For as liberality is a virtue, so prodigality is a vice. . . . The damage done by the squandering of former times is felt by us today – in the Reduction which has come upon us, in the jealousies within the Estate of Nobility, in the non-payment of wages – as the beginning of the ruin of the First Estate. And therefore for my second principle I advance that middle-term between vice and virtue, which is economy. For since men serve for honour and reward, we must always arrange matters so that we have the means of rewarding them at our disposal, and must suit our donations to the resources and incomes of the state, and not try to match the practice of other nations which have a hundred *daler* to our one. We should rather follow the example of former Kings, who when they wished to show favour to anyone bestowed upon them some tithes, or the income from fines in a local court, or exemption from taxes for life, and gave permanently tax-free land only to those of exceptional merit or devotion. . . . We who are Regents should exercise the more restraint in this, since what is done is subject to the King's ratification; . . . in particular I must as a Regent be scrupulous in declining any acquisition for myself which might be a bad example to others. And my maxim of economy must apply not only in regard to grants of land, but also in regard to the giving of monetary rewards . . . for no man of conscience could consent to deny a man his well-earned salary, or refuse payment to someone who has advanced money for the country's service, in order to bestow a gratification upon somebody else who could very well have been left without it. . . . There are only two ways of making the income of the state adequate to balancing the expenditure which its needs demand: one is cutting and pruning; the other is increasing the yield of the revenues. In cutting, we should look principally to the abolition of useless and inefficient offices, and we should graduate salaries according to merit and responsibility (and also according to what the crown can afford), and not according to social status. [Other economies, mainly military, are suggested.]

I find myself (by what destiny I know not) occupying the office of Treasurer – which, apart from all other anxieties, entails the hatred of all men . . . since however hard one tries it is not possible to content everyone, for *ex nihilo nihil fit*; and I must say that I am not surprised at their irritation, especially in the case of those who serve the state and receive no wages, which is contrary to the law of God, the law of Nature, and the law of every country. . . . It infects the country with what I can only call a hereditary disease. For hitherto we have made every effort to bring up our children to be fit to serve the state; we have spent all we had upon them, in hopes that they would recover the outlay when they were in a position to be honoured with an appointment under the crown; but now when they find that this is the case no longer, and that there is nothing to be earned in the crown's service, they change their views, quit the service, and try to earn a living in private life . . . and the result is like to be (as it has been before in this country) that we shall have to import foreigners to serve the state; and whoever they may be, they will certainly have to be paid. And however much we may afterwards try to repair the damage, and however much we spend in the effort, it will not be possible to do it; so that I hold it to be essential for the kingdom that every state-servant be paid his wage.

[For a kingdom to be flourishing, its subjects must flourish too. He proceeds to consider how each Estate may be made more prosperous.]

To take the Estate of Nobles first. . . . The principal interest of the Nobility consists in their being employed in the service of the state, and in having lands and farms to give them a livelihood, in conjunction with their wages; and these lands are a *sine qua non*, without which a nobleman cannot exist. For it does not become him, like the other three Estates, either to learn a craft, or to walk behind a plough, and sooner than do so he will betake himself to unlawful pursuits. And one of the conditions that helps to preserve the integrity of the Estate is that the Nobility shall not be so numerous that its members cannot all find civil or military employment to safeguard them from the disgrace of poverty. Consider what distress – and in some cases, ruin – has resulted from the great increase in recent times in the size of the Estate by the ennoblement of persons, some of whom deserved it, and some of whom did not; so that it has come about that many a boy must go into service to his equals, and old families (as well as more recent ones) go without employment, and estates must be broken up, so that but for the wars many a family would sink into poverty. . . . I say nothing of what is suffered by our old families, who see positions which in the past were given to them conferred upon men who have only recently been admitted to the peerage, while they themselves go without employment. And for this reason we should do well to confer peerages with a very sparing hand. . . . We should also try to persuade our old families to abandon the notion that they cannot permit recent peers to take precedence of them, and so refuse employment on that account. . . .

Of all the Estates, it is the Clergy who have succeeded best in maintaining their rights; and the only maxim I have in their regard is that the bishops should be discouraged from ordaining more clergy than can find speedy employment. . . . Also, that we should try to cultivate their goodwill, though not to the extent of allowing them to go beyond their proper sphere, or permitting them to meddle in politics or the affairs of government, as they are wont to do at Diets and elsewhere.

The Burghers are an Estate which draws its livelihood and nutriment from the three other Estates, and in return nourishes them again. [He proceeds to consider the perennial question of why urban development, industry and commerce are less advanced in Sweden than in western Europe.] When I look into it carefully, I find that the main cause is the action of the crown, which ruins all rich merchants in two ways: first, as soon as a man becomes rich, it makes him a peer, which means that he abandons commerce, puts his capital into land, and thereby ruins other members of the nobility – and even granting that he continues in commerce, it is only for his lifetime, for his children, instead of continuing the business, stick their money into land; with the result that we have no *entrepreneurs* to undertake manufactures. And secondly, the crown ruins them by defaulting on its debts. . . .

As to the Peasantry, the most important point is that they should be secured, like the other Estates, in their lawful rights and their ancient liberties as freeholders . . . for it is better to milk the cow than to hit it over the head. Anything that can be done to spare them the quartering or passage of troops contributes much to their well-being, and there is no doubt that if the peasant is treated well he will remain in a good humour and improve his condition, provided God is pleased to grant us good harvests.

Printed, with commentary by Georg Wittrock, in *Historisk Tidskrift*, XXXIII (1913), pp. 43–4, 46–54

XXIX The Reduction, 1680

During Karl XI's minority the Reduction College had continued in sluggish activity, the crown's recoveries being largely offset by new alienations. The lower Estates had not forgotten the crisis of 1650, nor dropped their demand for a revival of the Reduction (extract (*a*)); and the financial crisis precipitated by the wars with Brandenburg and Denmark gave new force to their arguments. As the number of peasants who paid rents or taxes to the nobility (instead of to the crown) increased, the fiscal burden on those that remained increased also. On the other hand, freehold peasants whose dues and services had been alienated to the nobility became increasingly discontented with their lot: after 1652 it seems that they had on the whole been *better* off than peasants of the nobility, or crown peasants; but the war had laid such burdens on them that this was no longer true. The war had indeed borne heavily on the nobility also: their fiscal immunities were repeatedly infringed, though always with their consent. At the Halmstad Diet of 1678 some of them began to demand a Reduction as a means of safeguarding themselves from paying taxes (extracts (*b*) and (*c*)). The connexion between such ideas and an emergent theory of absolutism is revealed in extract (*d*). When the Diet met in 1680 the King's supporters (against their better knowledge) encouraged the Nobility to believe that a Reduction would ensure their fiscal immunity for the future. Jealousy of the lesser nobility for the great magnates; a desire for vengeance on the Regents; the royalists' dislike of the Council's constitutional pretensions; a widespread feeling that the safety of the country demanded that the crown should be financially strong; and most of all, perhaps, the desire of noble office-holders that the crown should be in a position to pay their wages with regularity (extract (*e*)) – all these helped to persuade the Nobility to accept a Reduction which they mistakenly supposed would this time be final (extract (*f*)).

(*a*)

Minutes of the Estate of Clergy, 15 September 1675

Dr Terserus reminded the Estate that in the answer which we were to make to H.M. something must be included about the Reduction, so that the resolution taken by the Diet in 1655 might be put into effect. . . .

At this point a deputation of eight persons from the Estate of Peasants delivered the text of what they had agreed upon in reply to the King's Proposition, namely, 1. Since tax- and crown-peasants are now mostly brought under the nobility, so that soon H.M. will have no peasants of his own at all to whom he can turn in time of need, that H.M. will be pleased to take into his hands the lands which formerly belonged to the crown. 2. The nobility have appropriated, for their own selfish purposes, the most useful of the extraordinary aids levied for carrying on the war. . . . And since the nobility are not the only persons who defend the country, fit out the fleet, and repair the fortresses, the commonalty takes it ill that all the crown's revenues are alienated, and that wherever an emergency occurs H.M. is forced tc lay burdens on those who are poor, and unable to bear them. They therefore supplicate that all aids which from time to time have beer granted to the crown shall be paid to the crown alone, so that the destitute and impoverished classes be not further burdened with them 3. That conscription for the army shall be applied equally to freeholders crown-peasants, and peasants of the nobility. . . .

Prästeståndets riksdagsprotokoll, iii, 218-19 220-1

(*b*)

Minutes of the Estate of Nobility, 7 February 1678

The discussion then turned to the many great aids which were levied and the abuses committed by the bailiffs and constables who collectec them. . . .

Herr Mauritz Posse: It is reasonable that we should all give ou assistance, but it must be made clear that we cannot all bear equa burdens, for we are not all equally well off. It would be a good thing i we could hit upon some means whereby we could escape having tc pay the contribution and at the same time protect our privileges from infringement. There are many who sit tight on alienated crown-lands and -revenues: as long as they *remain* alienated, we can never hope tc escape contributions, nor be sure of keeping our privileges intact. He hoped that his words would not give offence: he meant well. But he asked leave to outline what he would suggest in the present instance. That all land intended for the support of the army should be returned to the crown. That Halland, Blekinge and Skåne, together with Bohuslän, be reserved to H.M., and no private person be allowed to occupy or draw advantage from lands which had been won for this country with such great efforts and expense, and at the cost of so much Swedish blood: such lands should be reserved for the good of the state, and not be allowed to pass into private hands. . . .

Svenska ridderskaps och adels riksdagsprotokoll, xii, 256

(*c*)

Minutes of the Estate of Nobility, 9 February 1678

. . . *Herr Mauritz Posse:* It is a hard thing to apply conscription to our home-farms. What then becomes of our privileges? It may well be that what we need is a new Reduction. What has happened to the army-lands?

Herr Bengt Rosenhane: No point in talking of a new Reduction until this one is finished, and we see how far it goes.

The Marshal: A new Reduction is a question for the whole Diet. If the previous one were being acted on it would be time enough to talk of another. . . .

Herr Mauritz Posse: Is it reasonable that we who have lands that have been in the family for years should pay contributions like the rest?

Herr Clas Fleming and others: It is no light matter when lands are reclaimed from one and then given to someone else.

Others: They take them away from those who have earned them by good service, and give them to others who don't deserve it.

Others thought that the Reduction ought to have been completed by this time.

. . . .

Herr Mauritz Posse said that this King could start a new Reduction of his own.

The Marshal: Yes, provided it is according to law, and with the Nobility's consent.

Gyllencrantz thought that no Reduction could go any further than this one: it would be an impossibility.

Others: since a Reduction would be based on necessity, it could very well go further. . . .

Ibid., 264–5, 267

(*d*)

Minutes of the Estate of Nobility, 21 February 1678

Herr Hans Wachtmeister thought that H.M. could not give confirmation of ownership for any land until the Reduction was over.

But others answered that those who were not involved in the Reduction ought not therefore to be prevented from getting security of tenure for their estates.

Herr Wachtmeister: What security? All estates come from the sovereign; though we may not know how.

Ibid., 290

(e)

Minutes of the Estate of Nobility, 29 October 1680

Herr Hans Wachtmeister: H.M.'s intention is that the budget may be put on a sound basis, and fixed at such a figure that it will not have to be revised, as has been the case in previous years. If this can be done by a contribution, I cannot tell; for my part, I should think it was impossible.

. . . .

Herr Per Sparre once again called attention to the fact that H.M.'s Proposition made no mention of any Reduction, but simply asked for financial support.

. . . .

Herr Conrad Gyllenstierna. Salus publica summa lex est; we know that the country is in desperate straits, and that everyone serves without wages, and that a handful of persons own all the land in the kingdom.

. . . .

Herr Christopher Gyllenstierna: Contributions won't get us anywhere; and in any case they are not properly paid.

Others: And what happens is that the poor among us have to pay up, but the rich and powerful, who own the nation's land, have done nothing: this is something which ought to be looked into.

. . . .

Herr Per Sparre: We have H.M.'s Proposition; it says nothing of a Reduction; and it is not for us to depart from it.

. . . .

The Marshal: We have been debating what we can do to help the country: the King has shown us what a great deficit there is on the budget. From this there now arises, incidentally, the question of a Reduction, and we may therefore now debate whether the country is to be helped out of its predicament by the methods formerly used, or by a new Reduction.

Herr Ekeblad: It seems rather difficult to express a view until we have first heard the opinion of the Council, and conferred with them. And he asked also that any decision might be taken in the manner prescribed in the Ordinance for the House of the Nobility.[1]

Herr Hans Wachtmeister: The resolution of the Halmstad Diet [of 1678] points the way. The overseas provinces must support themselves: they should be the bastions of the realm, and not a burden on it; and therefore they must be brought back into public ownership by a Reduction. . . . If that were done, the provinces would probably not only be able to pay for themselves, but have a sizeable surplus for other needs. Skåne, Halland, Blekinge and Bohuslän are the outworks which defend the realm against all attackers: as long as they are not recovered into public hands the country will not be safe; and it is out of the question to expose it to the danger it is in at present for the sake of a few persons.

. . . .

Herr Per Sparre: If anything is to be done, it should be done in an orderly fashion. Let us first find out how much is involved in the donated lands: it may well be that they would not make all that difference.

The Marshal again reminded them that the Classes should now give their decisions.

Herr Axel Wachtmeister objected that this was not a matter that could be voted on.

Herr Hans Wachtmeister: We must at once make our grant without voting.

. . . .

At this point there was a loud hum of discussion in the Classes, which lasted a considerable time; after which Col. *Örneklo* delivered the opinion of the Third Class: the view of the Third Class was (1) that the Resolution of the Diet of 1655 must be carried out without any impediment; (2) that the Resolutions of 1678 and 1672 must likewise be carried out in the conquered provinces; (3) that the great fiefs and other donations of land must be restored to the crown, without respect of persons, and whatever their date; (4) and as all grace derives from the King, so the Nobility humbly seek the King's protection, beseeching

[1] *The Riddarhusordning* of 1626, which regulated procedure in the house. Ekeblad was demanding secret voting, in order to protect members from royal displeasure (*cf.* p. 73, above). He did not get it: to the fury of the conservatives the Marshal steadily refused to agree to it.

him to preserve the privilege of their Estate [*sc.* its immunity from taxation], and to provide them with such means of support as may serve to the maintaining of their Order.

Governor Mårten Reutercrantz, in amplification, said: On this side too most of us are of the same opinion, though we would add to the point about H.M.'s preserving of privileges, that any man whose revenues are 600 *daler* (silver) or less should be allowed to retain those revenues: any excess above 600 *daler* to revert to the crown; and that lands which have been acquired from the crown by purchase, or as security, should not be touched.

Opinion of the Second Class. *Herr Axel Wachtmeister:* The Second Class is of the same opinion as the Third Class. . . .

Judge Ulf Bonde and *Governor Axel Stålarm* leapt to their feet, saying that this was not the opinion of the Class, and that the Class had not known what was really being proposed. To which *Herr Axel Wachtmeister* and *Col. Soop* retorted that this was the Class's agreed view.

At that *Herr Hans Wachtmeister*, in the First Class, sprang to his feet, saying: All those of us who are for the Reduction gather round, and we'll go up to the King. And therewith took some steps across the floor.

Col. Erik Soop then leapt up in the Second Class, clapped his hat on his head and brandished his stick, shouting: Come on! Let's go!

At the same moment *Herr Per Sparre* jumped up, saying: We can go to the King just as well as you!, and moved with some others to the door.

Then *Herr Hans Wachtmeister*, and the others who were of his opinion, turned back and resumed their seats; but *Herr Per Sparre*, *Col. Count Karl Oxenstierna*, *Count Frederick Stenbock*, *Admiral Horn*, and others, went quickly out of the hall and up to the Castle. *The Marshal* ordered the Secretary to go after *Herr Sparre* and the others, and beg them to come back; which the Secretary did, but they excused themselves, and continued on their way. . . .

Thereupon *The Marshal* asked the Classes to resume their seats, and urged the Estate to turn its mind to the welfare of the country, agree among themselves, and bring the matter to a proper conclusion. . . .

To this Col. *Örneklo* replied that since the Classes were now in agreement there could be no doubt that the Reduction was approved in principle, but that there must be further discussion about the method.

Herr Hans Wachtmeister rose and protested against those who had left the House, and so tried to put obstacles in the way of something which all the Estates had found to be for the service of H.M. and the kingdom.

Ibid., xiii, 71–2, 75–7

Minutes of the Estate of Nobility, 5 November 1680

Herr Hans Wachtmeister thought it was unreasonable that those who have accepted crown land instead of wages should retain it; and pointed out that those who had had no wages now for many years had served quite as honourably as the former, although they had received no crown lands as payment; and he thought such acquisition of crown lands in place of wages ought not to be held valid.

Governor Mårten Reutercrantz, on the contrary, considered that wages were of such a nature that a master was bound to pay his servants; and that a servant was consequently entitled to demand his wages, just like any other debt. . . .

Herr Per Sparre: If the King were to pay everybody who has a claim for wages, he would have nothing left.

Herr Hans Wachtmeister: There are wages and wages. Is it reasonable to claim one's wages for many years back, and get crown lands for them?

Others: In former years many people have deliberately neglected to draw their wages, so that they might have their pick of crown lands later on.

Others: There should be a time-limit set, after which it is not possible to buy crown lands with one's arrears.

To which others answered: You can't fix any definite time, for all are equally entitled to their wages. If one is to lose, others must lose too; otherwise it is most unfair.

Ibid., xiii, 115

. . . .

(*f*)

The Reply of the Estate of the Nobility to H.M.'s Proposition, 20 November 1680

. . . We have therefore, most gracious King, of our own motion, and out of our devotion to Y.M. and to the welfare of these realms, consented to a Reduction, upon the following terms:

That all counties and baronies, whether given before or after the year 1604 . . . and upon whatsoever conditions, shall with their revenues for the next coming year 1681 be entirely restored to Y.M. and to the crown, and the lands contained in them resume their original character.[1] In the same manner we consider that all crown farms or manors, at whatever time or upon whatever terms they may have been donated . . . shall be reduced (together with their revenues for the year 1681) according to the tenour of the statute of 1655.

. . . .

And that Y.M. may more fully perceive the Nobility's zeal for the welfare of crown and country, they have been willing to go further, even though they believe that they have already given a great and effective proof of their determination to come to Y.M.'s assistance; for they have in addition agreed, and do now grant, that all lands held in terms of the resolution of the Diet of Norrköping (**XIX**) . . . shall, with their next year's revenue, revert to the crown in respect of all income in excess of 600 *daler* (silver), *per annum*; but when the income does not exceed 600 *daler* (silver), the Nobility shall retain it without question, so that the donatee may enjoy up to 600 *daler* income undisturbed, upon the Norrköping terms.

. . . .

Since there may well be members of the Nobility who have bought crown land, the Estate humbly entreats Y.M. that such persons may without let or hindrance be protected in the possession of their purchases, in all cases where the sale was made by the Kings of Sweden themselves, or where it has been confirmed by them, or has been already cleared by the Reduction. But the Nobility likewise feel called upon to represent to Y.M. that such purchases as are not found to be authorized by any of the aforesaid warranties should be most carefully investigated . . . , and that where it is found that the estate was bought for ready money, and paid for in cash, the purchaser be permitted to remain in undisturbed possession. But for those who obtained lands of the crown against loans of various kinds, or pensions, or wages, there should be a careful and thorough audit, and the result be referred to the gracious pleasure and judgment of Y.M. But on the other hand no person should be disquieted, and still less disturbed in possession, who has had *bona fide* [commercial] dealings with the crown, until

[1] i.e. either as crown land, or as land subject to tax.

after strict scrutiny his accounts have been paid and his claims fully satisfied.

The Nobility are of opinion that the advantage of Y.M. and the country require that there be rigorous enquiry into the lands which have from time to time been mortgaged by the crown, with a view to discovering whether or not the crown received ready money in return: if so, then the mortgagee should retain possession in full security until he has been paid in full, care being taken to make sure that the revenues of the mortgaged land are not in excess of the ordinary rate of interest at 8 per cent. . . . Should it be found that the land has been mortgaged against goods and commodities, then definite rules should be laid down for estimating the crown's indebtedness, and particular care should be taken that goods and commodities be assigned no more than their value according to the official price-lists, and no claim shall be allowed from those who have bought up old bills, and have had crown land mortgaged to them in exchange for such bills.

. . . .

From this Reduction, and all other inquisition, the Estate of Nobility exempt and reserve all their allodial and hereditary estates descending in the male or female line, so that . . . their owners may be free of all apprehension, now and in the future.

. . . .

And whereas the Estate of Nobility have thus, of their own mere motion, and out of the zeal and affection which they bear towards Y.M., consented to this Reduction, so they do it in the full conviction that they will not hereafter, at any future time, be solicited to grant any further Reduction, which they herewith accordingly declare themselves never in any shape to be prepared to accept or undergo; but they expect rather, and most humbly beg, that Y.M. will from this Resolution cause such assurance for the future to be drawn that no further Reduction than this which is now so unanimously granted shall ever be proposed to them, nor they be considered in duty bound to submit to one; and that Y.M. may be most graciously pleased to give them such a general confirmation and guarantee of their allodial, hereditary, and Norrköping-resolution lands, as may safeguard them, now and for all future ages, from any new Reduction or other investigation.

The Estate of Nobility make it their humble request to Y.M. that those who have hitherto possessed the lands which are now to be reduced, may be permitted the opportunity of leasing them, in preference to any other persons.

. . . .

And the Estate of Nobility presume that when all this has been executed and properly carried out, the country will have thereby been given such powerful assistance that it will be possible hereafter for Y.M.'s subjects to be relieved of the necessity to make contributions.

Ibid., pp. 342 *seqq.*

XXX The origins of the Reduction, as seen by a victim

The Reduction was carried out with ruthless severity: it affected the innocent and the meritorious no less than the undeserving and the crooked speculators in the crown's necessities; the King did not hesitate to break the pledged word of himself and his predecessors; and his agents showed a refined ingenuity in discovering pretexts for establishing royal claims. Among the high aristocracy, who were hardest hit, it produced understandable bitterness, of which this account (by one of them) is a fair sample. It is true that the seventies had seen sharp party struggles among the men who surrounded the King; it is true, too, that some of the new men who triumphed in the years after 1680 had by no means clean hands; but the extract is to be taken not so much as an adequate explanation of why the Reduction occurred, as the reflection of the feelings it induced in its victims.

In those days, when the flames of war began to be kindled on all hands; . . . it was determined, on the pretext of the coronation, that a Diet should be summoned to Uppsala in the autumn [of 1675], and should there acclaim and anoint the young King according to law; and at the same time should take certain decisions for the prosecution of the war . . . and the provision of the money requisite for it. But in truth the object was to lay the basis for those measures which have subsequently proved so fatal to the Council, the entire nobility, and in particular to the older families; measures of which the effects will not easily be effaced, unless God should intervene to turn back the current of events.

In this connection, something has been said already of the parties at

Court. They had long been rivals for the King's ear, and had long sought to ruin those whose former places they were now occupying. The ambitions and mutual jealousies which animated these parties thus had as their consequence the discrediting in the eyes of the King not only of the Chancellor [Magnus Gabriel de la Gardie], but also of the greater part of the Council; and in their place the lower order of persons won all the favours they could ever have aspired to, and ought therewith to have been satisfied. But as the King's favour also opened the door to greed and luxury, they saw the chance to live in the same grand style of housing, furniture, equipages, food and drink, as their predecessors had used; though the latter had for the most part inherited from many generations resources which enabled them to stand the financial strain, while the new men found themselves short of money. They wished to see their families established, and hence they sought every means to enrich themselves; but the wages of the minor offices which they had hitherto held did not take them very far, and they did not venture to ask for financial aid from the King, since that would expose them to the same charge of self-interest, and of living grandly at the public expense, which they had launched against those they had supplanted.... They were therefore driven to devise other means, lawful or unlawful, caring nothing for the methods they employed, and careless if the very bases of the state should be overthrown or turned upside down, provided only that they could get what they wanted. The principal means they employed to compass their ends was so to arrange things that all private property was involved in such uncertainty that no man could be sure of his most insignificant possession, no matter whether he had acquired it by favour of former monarchs and the services of his ancestors, or by his own thriftiness and ingenuity; but that all was to depend upon the King's grace, and that no subject was to have such a title that the King was not able to deprive him of it with some show of legality, and give it away to whomsoever he would. And as these gentry now stood nearest the King, it would be hard if they should fail to secure the choicest pickings.... In order to effect their purpose, therefore, ... they had recourse first to the implementation of the Reduction granted in 1655, as a forerunner of another which was to be even more extensive; and in 1673 had the inalienable lands immediately resumed by the crown ... in terms of the Diet's Resolution of 1655. But as these simple reclamations of royal gifts were not sufficient for their purposes, they ... imitated the conduct of the Roman general in Italy, who after the death of Widikind, King of the

Goths, under the pretext of scrutinizing the accounts presented by the King's servants for the services they had rendered, took from them all that they had, and brought them to the sharpest destitution, to his own great enrichment. For they argued that since the King's coffers were now empty by reason of the lavish outpourings of former times, some means must be provided to ensure that the present King should have the wherewithal to reward his faithful servants; since no government can be conducted, nor any man be got to serve it, without rewards and punishments. Why, then, should we not go to work by methods which are still everyday practice in Turkey, where the Sultan treats his subjects as though they were leeches; which, once they are full, must spew out the blood they have sucked in, and so be reduced to first principles – that is, to being poor miserable slaves. If this is right for one nation, why not for another — provided only that it seems to pay. For in matters of politics, and where reasons of state are in question, honesty must give way to utility. No account need be taken of any objections which might be raised by the Clergy: they can be induced to avert their eyes by talk of 'the public interest'; and the more readily since their own private advantage is involved, which is a thing this species of humanity will never lose sight of. For they can be encouraged to hope that by these means they may be able to safeguard their own property, which would otherwise be eaten up with taxes; and this delusion will serve also to lull the other Estates, so that they will gladly lend a hand to the task of hacking broad strips from somebody else's hide, provided they can keep their own skin intact. As to the King, it could be of no consequence to him whether the old families were flourishing or not, since the true nobility consisted in innate virtue and ability, and not in birth; and the King would therefore never lack the support of the peerage, for men of ability would always be found among the offspring of other Estates, who could be employed by the King and give him better service than he would get from members of families which were so ancient that they had grown rotten. But it was for the King alone to have in his hands the property of every man, and he could therefore hand out his favours either by simply leaving a man in peace, or by giving him something for himself; and, finally and most important of all, there was no man in the Kingdom who did not owe his good fortune to the King, and enjoy it by his grace. These were indeed dangerous counsels . . . and they produced that general revolution which is now an accomplished fact. It has neither enriched nor advantaged anyone, either in general or in particular, in the same degree as it has inflicted hurt. That hurt we are now experiencing; and it will be many, many years before it can be repaired, if indeed it can ever be repaired at all.

Carl Bonde: *Anecdoter uti Sweriges historia;* printed in *Anteckningar om Bondesläkten,* ii, 143–8

C

FOREIGN AFFAIRS

XXXI Gustav Adolf on the Peace of Stolbovo, 1617

The peace of Stolbovo, which terminated Swedish intervention in Russia on very advantageous terms, was Gustav Adolf's first great political success. It deprived the dynastic enemy in Poland of access to the back-door to Sweden; it made Finland secure from Russian attacks; it excluded the Tsar from the Baltic. It is with these strategic gains that Gustav Adolf's speech is most concerned; but it refers also (though clearly as a secondary consideration) to the long-standing Swedish dream of controlling, and mulcting, the whole trade between Muscovy and the West, perhaps by channelling it through Narva. This was a delusion: trade would always find other ways round the Swedish customs-posts. The suggested colonization of Ingria received direct encouragement in the twenties by the transportation thither of unruly peasants, cutters-down of royal forests, and hunters of royal game.

Speech to the Estates at the opening of the Stockholm Diet, 26 August 1617

I cannot neglect to inform you of the great and splendid victory which Almighty God has given us against the Russians, and the glorious peace which has resulted from it. . . . It is indeed a thing worthy to be reckoned among God's miracles. For what could be more glorious than to have driven back this our mighty neighbour, with whom we have for ages lived side by side on uncertain terms and with precarious safety, so that he has been forced to yield up those robber-nests from which he was wont to espy us, and is now (by God's grace) divided from us by lakes, morasses and rivers over which he will not easily be able to pass to do us a mischief. In the past his near neighbourhood was hurtful to us, since he was so close at hand, and for the greater part of the length of the frontier on that side our lands marched with his: moreover, he had the advantage of convenient rivers with their numerous river-craft – rivers which rise deep within his best and most populous lands; and by their means it was very easy for him to concentrate his forces, and bring them downstream to fall upon us. . . .

Finland is now separated from Russia by the wide expanse of Lake Ladoga, which is as broad as the sea between Sweden and Åland, or between Estonia and Nyland – and over *that* no Pole so far has ventured. And I trust in God that in future it will be no easy matter for the Russian to leap such a ditch. And if he should get over it (which God forbid) the fortresses of Kexholm and Nöteborg – strong both by art and nature – should hold him up for a space, and bar his way into Finland. Estonia is protected by Narva and Ivangorod, as well as by the rapid river Narova, which rises in the beautiful Lake Peipus, and is no easy stream to overpass. Nor are Narva and Ivangorod easy to capture; and unless they be captured no soldier will be very anxious to venture to the other side of the Narova. . . . Ingria is protected on three sides by the Baltic, by Lake Ladoga and by Lake Peipus; and where it abuts on Russia is defended by vast swampy marshes, which divide Swedish territory from Muscovy. Lake Ladoga also covers the flank of a good deal of the fief of Kexholm, and of Karelia, and the latter runs up to the Arctic fells, where no army can pass. Thus it seems as though God had intended, in this hour of victory, to give us the protection of Nature itself against our false foe the Russian; for he cannot now launch a single boat (let alone a fleet) on the Baltic without our permission. Nöteborg lies athwart the Nyen; Ivangorod and Narva stand on either bank of the Narova, and past these he cannot come.

This peace, moreover, . . . means that the Swedish crown and those who wear it can now by God's providence order and prescribe as they choose in regard to the trade to Narva. It will be within the memory of many, how the Russians infringed our right to that trade when we were in no position to resent it. And we have never known how long we might enjoy that right unchallenged and without fear of attack from them. There has also been much dispute over it with other foreign nations, who chose to feel themselves affronted because we in some measure claimed to prescribe to them the terms upon which they should be permitted to trade there. . . . Now by this victory and the present peace all these difficulties are swept away, and the merchants and traders of our towns are once more presented with a centre in Narva for all the Russia trade, which has laid the basis and ensured the populousness of so many towns, and from which they too may now draw great profit and advantage. It is now open to them to carry on their trade, through Russia, to anywhere they please. . . .

. . . I say nothing of the great sums which could be collected by a fair and moderate toll upon trade, since the whole trade to Russia must now go through those lands; but it is clear that these territories are capable not only of bringing on our towns and much improving the revenues of the crown, but also of being a benefit to every one of our subjects. And so I say to you of the Nobility – and to you others too, who clamour for grants of land – what do you here, treading on each other's toes, quarrelling and wrangling for a few wretched farms? Be off with you to these new lands, and clear for yourselves farms as big as you like, or at least as large as you can manage! I will bestow privileges and immunities upon you; I will give you assistance; I will show you every favour.

Tal och skrifter av Konung Gustav II Adolf (ed. Carl Hallendorff), pp. 46–53

XXXII The Treaty of Bärwalde, 13 January (O.S.) 1631

The treaty of Bärwalde registers Richelieu's failure to hire Gustav Adolf as his mercenary. In return for French subsidies (important to Sweden at this stage of the war) Gustav Adolf made no reciprocal sacrifices, unless indeed his acceptance of the demolition of Spanish fortresses in the Grisons can be considered as such. Richelieu's hope of preventing a Swedish-Bavarian clash, and remaining friends with both powers, received no encouragement: indeed, the final words of extract (*b*) ('open or clandestine, against us and our friends and allies . . . [etc.]') virtually served notice on the Cardinal that his policy in this respect was bankrupt already.

(*a*)

[After a preamble]

Between Their Most Serene Majesties the Kings of Sweden and France there shall be an alliance for the defence of the friends of each and both of them, for the safeguarding of the Baltic and Oceanic Seas, the liberty of commerce, and the restitution of the oppressed States of the Roman Empire; and also in order to ensure that the fortresses and defence-works which have been constructed, in the ports and on the shores of the Baltic and Oceanic Seas, and in the Grisons, be demolished and reduced to the state in which they were immediately before this present German war. And because up to the present the enemy has refused to give a just reparation for the injuries he has caused, and has hitherto rejected all appeals, [the allies] take up arms to vindicate the cause of their common friends. To that end the King of Sweden . . . will at his own expense bring to and maintain in Germany 30,000 foot and 6000 heavy-armed cavalry. The King of France will contribute 400,000 Imperial *Thaler*, that is, a million *livres tournois*, every year, which will be paid and accounted for without fail to the agents of the King of Sweden deputed for that purpose, either at Paris or Amsterdam, as the King of Sweden may find the more convenient; whereof one half to be paid on 15 May, and the other on 15 November each year. The raising of soldiers and sailors, the sale of ships and materials of war, are to be free as between the territories of the allies, but are to be refused to enemies. . . . If God should be pleased to grant successes to the King of Sweden, he is in matters of religion to treat territories occupied by or ceded to him according to the laws and customs of the Empire; and in places where the exercise of the Roman Catholic religion exists, it shall remain undisturbed. Any other States or Princes, as well within Germany as without, who may wish to accede to this league, shall be admitted to it. . . . With the Duke of Bavaria and the Catholic League friendship, or at least neutrality, is to be preserved, provided that they on their side observe it. And if, by the grace of God, an opportunity to treat for peace should present itself, the negotiations shall be conducted jointly by the allies, and neither will without the other initiate or conclude a peace. This alliance shall last for five years . . . : if a sure peace is not obtained within that time, it may be further extended by agreement of the allies. It is agreed, finally, that since negotiations for this alliance began last year, and the King of Sweden has in the meanwhile been at great expense for this war, for this first year, which is now almost elapsed, 300,000 *livres tournois*, that is, 120,000 Imperial *Thaler*, shall be furnished in the name of the King of France on the day of the signature of this present treaty. . . .

(*b*)

Gustav Adolf's guarantee of neutrality for the Elector of Bavaria and the Catholic League, 15 January 1631

We, Gustavus Adolphus, by the Grace of God etc. Be it known to all men, that whereas the most serene and mighty Prince . . . Louis XIII . . . , our most dear Ally, has earnestly entreated us . . . to take especial care to observe friendship and neutrality, on a reciprocal basis, towards the . . . Elector of Bavaria and the Catholic League, we are therefore willing, out of our regard for the aforesaid Most Christian King, to indulge him, as our brother and ally, in this matter; so that the said . . . Elector of Bavaria and the Catholic League shall be safe from our enmity within their own territories, and shall enjoy an amicable neutrality, for so long as the said Elector of Bavaria and the Catholic League on their side sincerely perform their parts as friends and neutrals, and abstain from every kind of hostility, open or clandestine, against us and our friends and allies, and do not consent to any hostile decrees against us. . . .

Sverges traktater med främmande magter, V_1, 439–42

XXXIII Gustav Adolf and Germany, 1630–2

The most probable general explanation of the King's policies in Germany is that given by Oxenstierna in 1633, printed below as extract (*a*). His concern was necessarily to ensure that the dangers he sought to guard against did not recur: he wanted security (*assecuratio*) for the future. At first he thought of *assecuratio* in territorial terms, as a hold on (e.g.) Stralsund or Wismar (extracts (*b*), (*c*), (*g*)); but as the war developed he came increasingly to think of it in terms of a league of German princes, which should continue after the war as a precaution against a recurrence of danger. Such a league might be under the control of himself, as Director – a continuation of the 'absolute *Directorium*' over allied forces during the war on which he increasingly insisted (e.g. extracts (*e*), (*f*)); and for this the Swedish clientelage which he sought to impose on Mecklenburg and Brunswick might have paved the way (extracts (*g*), (*h*)). But it was at least conceivable that the league might be led by (e.g.) John George of Saxony (extract (*i*)). In the closing months of his life Gustav Adolf took steps to organize the nucleus of such a league in south-west Germany (extract (*j*): from this initiative the League of Heilbronn (**XXXIV**) was to develop. At the same time he developed his claim to compensation for Sweden's war-effort. At first he thought of this indemnity (*satisfactio*) as a cash payment, to be secured by retaining conquered places in his hand until it was paid (extracts (*e*), (*g*)); but gradually he came to think of it as implying permanent territorial cessions – of some Baltic ports, for instance, or possibly of Pomerania, whose acquisition was already seen as a contingency in the treaty with Bogislaw XIV (clause 14 of extract (*d*)): what had once been *assecuratio* came to be thought of as *satisfactio*. And it was with *satisfactio*, far more than with *assecuratio*, that Sweden's policy after 1634 was to be concerned (**XXXVI–XXXVII** below).

(*a*)

Minutes of Conference between Axel Oxenstierna and the Brandenburg government in Berlin, 30–31 January/9–10 February 1631

Concerning the King's Intentions

They were, in general, to disrupt the plans of the enemy, whose proceedings and intentions with regard to the Baltic are sufficiently well known. His Majesty therefore intended to ensure the safety of his kingdom and the Baltic, and to liberate the oppressed lands [of Germany]; and thereafter to proceed according as events might develop: it was no part of his original intention to press on as far as he did. . . . *Momenta temporum* were always the basis of his plans. . . . The King would have adapted his policies in the light of the enemy's action, the circumstances of the moment, and the conduct of his friends.

G. Irmer, *Die Verhandlungen Schwedens und seiner Verbündeten mit Wallenstein und dem Kaiser von 1631 bis 1634*, ii, 26–7

(*b*)

Debate in the Council, 4 May 1630

Whether it was advisable to restore Stralsund, in the event of the Emperor's accepting the terms proposed to him [at the Danzig conference]?

Herr Gabriel [*Gustafsson Oxenstierna*] thought that the question was settled by the terms of our treaty with Stralsund, since they laid it down that the King is to withdraw his garrison as soon as the Emperor restores the original state of affairs [in Mecklenburg]. . . .

The King: . . . Our basic war aim is security; and if the Emperor will grant the terms we have proposed, that would be a sufficient guarantee; but if the King were then to continue his occupation of Stralsund it would look as though he sought to enlarge his dominions. . . .

[Others] denied that this would be an adequate guarantee of safety; for if our security is to be assured it must be under our own control, and not in the discretion of the enemy, for . . . there can be no safety if we hand back any position which we cannot immediately retake. . . .

Herr Gabriel thought that we ought in the first place to demand a general restitution of the Estates [of Germany]. . . .

The King made the point that it would be iniquitous to deprive the Dukes of Pomerania and Mecklenburg of their hereditary rights for the sake of getting an agreement with the Emperor.

The Field-Marshal [*Jakob de la Gardie*]*:* It is quite possible for the King to occupy their lands without claiming dominion over them.

Svenska riksrådets protokoll, ii, 1-4

(*c*)

Gustav Adolf to Axel Oxenstierna, 12 May 1630

On Oxenstierna's draft of an instruction to the Swedish delegates at the Danzig negotiations

The King is well satisfied with the instructions as a whole, but notices that the Chancellor has omitted to bear in mind the most important point of all, namely *assecuratio*. The Chancellor is accordingly to take care that the King is not engaged to quit Stralsund, or any other place which he may be able to acquire, until all the conditions of peace are carried out by the Imperialists, their armies entirely withdrawn from the Saxon Circles, and everything (especially the coastlands) restored to a secure and peaceable condition.

Axel Oxenstiernas skrifter och brevvexling, II, i, 603-4

(*d*)

Treaty of alliance between Gustav Adolf and Bogislaw XIV of Pomerania, 10 July (O.S.) 1630

[1-2. The alliance to be eternal, renewable every ten years, and defensive.]

3. In the third place, this union is not directed against the majesty of the Emperor or the Empire, but is rather designed to maintain the constitution of the Empire in its ancient state of liberty and tranquillity, and to protect the religious and secular settlement against the ravages of the disturbers of the public peace, and thereby not only to leave intact the relationship which binds us, Bogislaw . . . to His Imperial Roman Majesty, and also to the Upper Saxon Circle, but also to preserve our lawful duty and obligations to the same. . . .

5. In the fifth place, such Pomeranian provinces, towns or fortified places as have been or in future shall be occupied by us, the King of Sweden, . . . shall at once be restored to the safe-keeping and due obedience of the Duke of Pomerania, without question, and without deduction of any war-expenses, and the town of Stralsund shall be enjoined to show a due respect for the Duke of Pomerania; while we, the Duke of Pomerania . . . will appoint such officials as will coöperate willingly with the Swedish commissaries in all that concerns the defence of the country; and will preserve the town of Stralsund in its privileges and its existing special alliance with the King.

14. Finally, and in the fourteenth place, we the King of Sweden have on our part made the express reservation that . . . should the Duke of Pomerania die without male heirs, before the Elector of Brandenburg . . . has ratified and confirmed this alliance and has given real assistance in the deliverance of these lands; or should the succession to Pomerania be contested by any other prince; we . . . or our successor on the throne, will take these lands into our sequestration and tutelage, until such time as the matter of the succession has been fully determined, and we have been indemnified by the successor for our war-expenses . . . , and this union and alliance has by him been duly ratified and implemented.

Sverges traktater med främmande magter V₁, 394–8

(*e*)

Draft treaty between Gustav Adolf and the Landgraves of Hesse-Cassel Stralsund, 11 November (O.S.), 1630

[1. Gustav Adolf takes the Landgraves under his 'care and protection' for the duration of the war; 4. promises that if he occupies their towns, their rights shall sustain no prejudice; 7. will send a deputy to command their joint forces if he cannot come himself, though 'reserving in all cases the absolute *directorium*' to himself; 10. will not exercise his rights 'as *caput* of this confederation' within the Landgraves' territories except in purely military matters.]

14. In the event of this or that place being occupied or taken by our armed forces (other than such places as are the Landgraves' property), the Landgraves will allow such occupied lands and places to remain in our hands until we have been indemnified for our war-expenses, and will collectively maintain us in the same.

Ibid., 495–503

(*f*)

Norma futurarum actionum, [*May 1631*]

The ultimate or supreme goal of all
Actions:
A new Evangelical Leader.
The penultimate objective:
A new league between the Evangelical Estates
and such a Leader.
This to be realized by the following
Means.

1

By a coördinated direction of the war; . . .

2

The foundation of it:
The right a patron has over his clients.

3

The confirmation of it

1. Lies in the concession . . . and occupation of fortified places.
2. By fixed contributions either to the expenses of the war, or of troops to be maintained at the charges of each member.
3. By free access to and transit through electorates, principalities, etc.
4. By denying requisitions to the enemy.

. . . .

9. By strong reciprocal agreements that neither party has the right without the knowledge and consent of the other to withdraw from this alliance until the ultimate objective of the war is within the reach of all.

B. Boëthius, 'Norma futurarum actionum', *Historisk Tidskrift* (1911), pp. 200–1

(*g*)

Gustav Adolf's alliance with the Dukes of Mecklenburg, 1631–2

(i) Gustav Adolf's draft of 17 September 1631

25. And if we, the King of Sweden, should by force of arms be able to make any conquest from our enemy . . . such conquest would be our rightful property, nor should we hold ourselves bound to restore it until at least we had been indemnified for the cost of this war; but for our own security only we will retain the town and harbour of Wismar, with the fort and harbour of Warnemünde, until we shall have further agreed about them with the Emperor.

(ii) The definitive treaty of 29 February (O.S.), 1632

II. And we the Dukes of Mecklenburg, having been restored to our rights and possessions, . . . and His Majesty the King of Sweden having taken us and our subjects and duchies into his tutelage and protection, we promise . . . thankfully to acknowledge the benefit conferred upon us [and to join forces with the Swedes], and further that we will never desert the King and his successors . . . in their need, whether it arise from this war or another. . . .

VII. And since nothing is more suitable to the present state of affairs than that His Majesty, who has come so far from his kingdom to restore his friends, should be assured of his return . . . , in order tha he may have in his power those places in our Duchies which are found to be suitable for naval stations, We the Dukes of Mecklenburg agree . . . hereby that His Majesty shall retain Wismar . . . and Warnemünde . . . saving our sovereignty of those places . . . up to the end ot this present war.

XI. . . . we hereby consent that His Majesty be permitted to impose tolls at Warnemünde and Wismar, and at the other ports and rivers of our Duchy; . . . on the understanding that one hundredth part of the said tolls be reserved to us.

XVIII. [To prevent all possible controversy] it is hereby laid down that . . . no objection based on former or future agreements or alliances, or ties of homage, shall have any force [against this alliance]; and especially we the Dukes of Mecklenburg, well considering that our restoration to our Duchies and our preservation in them depends upon His Majesty, hereby declare that the ties by which we are bound to the

Empire, or the Saxon Circle, or other of our neighbours, ought not and cannot stand in the way of, or prejudice, this our alliance. . . .

Sverges traktater med främmande magter, V_1, 718-19, 706-13

(*h*)

Gustav Adolf's draft treaty with Frederick-Ulric of Brunswick-Wolfenbüttel, December-January 1631/2

11. [Gustav Adolf promises to restore occupied places in the Duchies at the end of the war to the Duke or his heirs] when they [the heirs] have ratified this alliance and have similarly bound themselves by it, and provided they have not forfeited such lands by adopting a hostile attitude; in order to which the Duke of Brunswick undertakes to secure from his Estates that they will not accept or do homage to any future Duke unless he has accepted this alliance and confirmed it.

II.1. [The Duke promises, for himself and his heirs] not only to accept the King of Sweden . . . for our ally and Protector, but also to respect and honour his heirs and successors . . . as such.

II.2. [The Duke engages to contract no alliance repugnant to this without the knowledge and consent of the King of Sweden, and to make no separate peace] until and unless a Royal Satisfaction has been accorded to His Majesty in recognition of his expenses, his victories, and *juris belli*.

J. Kretzschmar, *Gustav Adolfs Pläne und Ziele in Deutschland*, pp. 258-62

(*i*)

Gustav Adolf's instruction for his envoy to John George of Saxony, Donauwörth, 1/11 June 1632

11. A principal question . . . to be considered, is how that most necessary and indispensable *corpus*, which must be the basis and guarantee of peace, can be founded upon a sound footing and organized under a single direction. His Majesty, for his part, considers that it would not be difficult to devise the means for creating a solid *corpus*, and is prepared to come forward with suggestions. It might be better, however, that the Elector himself should first make known his views as to whether he intends to consider His Majesty's personal participation, and to declare

whether he intends that such a *corpus* should be governed and guided by His Majesty, and be under his absolute direction . . . , or whether he intends to satisfy His Majesty's claims and permit him to retire; or again whether he proposes to draw closer his ties . . . with the crown of Sweden, or whether the idea is to put up a leader among themselves, and entrust the direction of the *corpus* to him.

Irmer, i, 207

(*j*)

Gustav Adolf's Memorandum for Oxenstierna's negotiation with the states of the Suabian, Franconian, and Upper and Lower Rhenish Circles, at the meeting to be held at Ulm. [*24(?) October 1632*]

1. Since the state of affairs in general, and especially the prosecution of the war against our formidable enemy, demands a close cohesion between those who are concerned for the common cause in Germany, as well as armies for defence and for carrying on the war into the enemy's country, together with financial resources sufficient to maintain them and to preserve military discipline, H.M. has resolved to call together the Estates of the four Circles to Ulm, and has charged his Chancellor Axel Oxenstierna to represent to them on H.M.'s behalf the present condition of affairs . . . and thus by gentle means to try to induce them deliberately to join together in defence of their welfare, and of the common cause, and to find means to translate their resolve into action.

2. In matters of form the Chancellor is to accommodate himself as well as he can to their customs and susceptibilities; but in matters of substance he is to make every effort to secure these three points: (1) to do all he can to induce them to break away from the Emperor, to acknowledge him no longer, and either directly . . . or indirectly to renounce him, and instead to bind themselves more closely to H.M., and to come under his direction and protection; (2) to join together to prosecute the war against the Emperor and his adherents . . . ; (3) last and most important, that they devise means whereby the armies which H.M. has planned and ordered may be supported and discipline preserved.

3. The Chancellor may permit a free discussion, and may hear what they propose; but sooner or later, as may be most appropriate, he is to suggest to them the example of the United Netherlands . . . [and also to suggest raising money by an excise on wine, beer, bread and meat].

7. If the Estates coöperate heartily, or at any rate tolerably, the Chancellor shall also . . . suggest that the Imperial Chamber of Justice in Speyer be entirely reconstituted. . . . But if he finds the Estates shy of this idea, he is not to raise the question, but to leave it to H.M. to bring forward at the appropriate moment; though he is to take every opportunity to have the Imperial President of the court, or other suspect persons, removed from the Imperial Chamber of Justice, and to make preparations for future changes.

Axel Oxenstiernas skrifter och brevvexling, II, i, 866–8

XXXIV The League of Heilbronn, 13 April 1633

After Gustav Adolf's death, Oxenstierna was able to organize the league of princes which Gustav Adolf's last plans had contemplated. His success was mostly confined to south-west Germany, for there the Protestant Estates were most obviously dependent on Swedish help. He never, however, succeeded in extending it to include Saxony and Brandenburg, and without them it was doomed to be a rump of Swedish puppets. The disaster at Nördlingen smashed it; the peace of Prague disintegrated it. Note the care, in clauses 1 and 9, to bind the allies to secure to Sweden her *satisfactio*.

After a preamble which recalls Gustav Adolf's intention of summoning the Estate of the Swabian, Franconian and Upper and Lower Rhenish Circles to a meeting in Ulm (**XXXIII**(*j*)), and states that that intention had now been implemented by Oxenstierna, the treaty of confederation follows.

First and foremost, the Princes and Estates who are present, and the envoys and delegates of those who are absent . . . do, for themselves, their heirs and successors, confederate with the crown of Sweden . . . ; and they agree that all the confederates shall be faithful, and give assistance, the one to the other . . . ; and that they will venture their persons, their lives and their fortunes in the cause, until such time as the liberties of Germany, and a respect for the principles and constitution of the Holy Roman Empire, are once again firmly established, the restoration of the Protestant Estates is secured, and a just and certain peace, in spirituals and temporals . . . is obtained and concluded, and also until the crown of Sweden has been assured of an appropriate satisfaction.

In the second place: the Estates and ambassadors here present, having come to the conclusion that the military organization cannot function without a competent supreme Director; and remembering that His late Majesty, . . . the saviour of German liberties, filled that position in his lifetime . . . have determined to show their respect to His late Majesty and to his Successor, and also to give a testimony of their high esteem of the Chancellor's excellent qualities, by asking and entreating him to take upon himself the office of Director . . . for the good of the common cause in its hour of need. . . .

In the third place: Since however the burden upon His Excellency the Director would be very heavy for him to bear unaided, it has been found good to provide him with a Standing Council of well-qualified persons, furnished with detailed instructions, with whose approval the Director . . . is to decide in all matters of importance; provided, however, that in military matters the final decision shall always remain with the Director himself.

[4-5. No separate negotiations for peace]

In the sixth place, it is agreed that for the duration of the present war, and until a secure peace is obtained conformable to our desires, the confederates in the four Circles will maintain the necessary armies, and provide them with pay, provisions, ammunition and artillery. . . .

. . . .

In the eighth place, His Excellency the Director has declared that he will take care, with the Council, that the militia is duly reformed; that the staffs of the other troublesome regiments are cut down; that military discipline is restored; that commerce, private trading and industry shall once more be put on a firm footing; that the jurisdiction of the ordinary courts shall be preserved, as well in criminal cases as in civil, so that they may punish all outrages except those committed in the course of military operations; that the excesses of the soldiery, as far as the times will allow, shall be suppressed; that good order shall be kept in quartering and marching, and the confederates, if at all possible, be spared; and that the allotment of quarters shall be left to the magistrates in each locality. And in return all the Estates undertake to take such measures in their territories as may ensure that the soldiery have adequate pay.

In the ninth place, the Estates and ambassadors here present, considering how not only His late Majesty in his day, but the crown of Sweden afterwards, have been so ready to offer them assistance, and indeed to continue it, have engaged to His Excellency the Director that in return they will help the aforesaid crown to keep possession of those enemy lands within the Empire which it already occupies, until the war is over, and a proper satisfaction is afforded; as also to take care that reasonable indemnity may be provided for the injuries sustained by others of the confederation.

Finally: as the confederation now concluded in the name of God has been a measure forced upon them by the great insolences of the enemy, and is designed as a legitimate measure of self-defence, and by no means as an offensive measure against any peace-loving state, so also it is a measure of moderation, implying no violation of the fundamental principles of the Holy Roman Empire, nor any infringement of the constitution or the Empire or the Circles, or of any sovereignties, dignities, superiorities or rights within them; nor does it intend any prejudice to those Electors and Estates who are loyal to the Empire, nor to any foreign potentate or republic. And the Confederates cherish the confident hope that to other Evangelical Electors and Estates of the Empire, and also to foreign potentates and republics, this work of salvation . . . will be not repugnant, but positively welcome, and that they will take occasion to adhere to and enter so Christian . . . a league. . . .

Sverges traktater med främmande magter, V_2, 18–19

XXXV–XXXVI Defeatism and Disengagement, 1635–6

The years 1634 and 1635 were years of disaster. In August 1634 the Swedes sustained the crushing defeat of Nördlingen; in September came a breach with Brandenburg; in November Saxony signed the Preliminaries of Pirna, which in May 1635 became the Peace of Prague. Within a few months the League of Heilbronn was in ruins, and virtually all Sweden's former German allies, save William V of Hesse-Kassel, had accepted the peace. In July, Oxenstierna was for a time the prisoner of his mutinous officers in Magdeburg. The Truce of Altmark expired this year, and the Council, terrified at the idea of a renewal of the Polish war, in May concluded (under French pressure) the Truce of Stuhmsdorf, whereby (to Oxenstierna's bitter indignation) they surrendered Prussia (and the vital tolls at the Prussian ports) in return for a 26-years' breathing-space. In October Saxony declared war; and in the same month Bernard of Saxe-Weimar and his army deserted the Swedish for the French service. A feeling of defeatism had for some time been growing in the Council, and Oxenstierna's political adversaries were accusing him of preventing a peace: to them was now added Salvius, Oxenstierna's former client, who had been sent home in 1633 to reinforce the Chancery. The strength of these feelings appears in the extracts printed in **XXXV**. Oxenstierna's return home in July 1636 coincided with a recovery from this loss of nerve; and the forces liberated from Prussia by the truce would soon enable Baner to win the crucial victory of Wittstock in September. A more balanced estimate of Sweden's chances now became possible: it is printed below, as **XXXVI**(*a*). It reveals for the first time the importance of what was destined to be one of the greatest obstacles to a final peace – the problem of how to pay off the armies' arrears. It makes clear, too, the tenacity with which Swedish statesmen struggled to hang on to a *satisfactio* which should be *territorial*. Oxenstierna had renewed the alliance with France at Wismar, in 1636; but he had taken good care not to ratify it, realizing that to do so would destroy all hope of a separate peace. The failure of that hope, and the need for French money, eventually led to the renewal of the alliance by the treaty of Hamburg in 1638: Oxenstierna's lack of enthusiasm for the connexion appears in **XXXVI**(*b*).

XXXV Defeatism, 1635

From the Minutes of the Council of the Realm

(*a*)

17 September 1635. Discussion as to what is to be written to the Chancellor [Axel Oxenstierna – still in Germany], and whether it would not be advisable for him frankly to pull out of Germany by degrees, and devote his efforts to doing it without loss of security and reputation, and without forfeiting German good-will: if he can secure something over and above, so much the better. The view was that if the Chancellor should win a victory, we may no doubt hope for reasonable peace-terms; if he loses a battle, he will be forced to retire northwards to a place of safety. In the meantime that he keep in close touch with the French, so that he may shape his conduct according to how things develop. He should make every effort to hang on to the most important places, as far as he can.

Decided that the Chancellor is to abide by Her Majesty's former instructions. If he can obtain any territory [at a supposititious peace], that would be best; if not, to take satisfaction in money; and if he cannot get that, to try every means consistent with reputation and safety to extricate himself from the German business.

Svenska riksrådets protokoll, v, 76

(*b*)

9 October. Discussion whether the news that the Elector of Saxony and the German Princes have separated themselves from us shall be publicly laid before the Estates. The view was that a gloss must be put upon it, and the information be conveyed in softened terms. . . . Since the Elector of Saxony wants to drive us out of Germany by force, it is plain that we must prepare to defend ourselves, in particular by providing garrisons and ample supplies for the coastlands, since our main armies are steadily falling back nearer and nearer to the coast.

Herr Per Baner urged that we could not simply get out of Germany, as once the King of Denmark did: he could see nothing for it but that we must fight.

Count Per Brahe said that we could not accept compensation in money, and preserve our honour. If the crown of Sweden could obtain satisfaction in land, that would be the best solution. . . . In any case our armies could hardly be paid off for less than 4 or 5 millions. It would seem best, therefore, if we cannot reach any respectable agreement with the Emperor, that we go on fighting. If we win a victory, we must exploit it; if we are beaten, then that disposes of the soldiers' arrears, and we can defend the strong places on the coast with the survivors.

Ibid., 192-3

(*c*)

10 October. *The Court Chancellor* [Johan Adler Salvius] gave the Regents his views about the possibility of negotiation with the Elector of Saxony, to the effect that since the Elector is hardly likely to be willing to let us arrange a general peace, he will try to prevent our negotiating directly with the Emperor, with whom he (and he alone) has made his dishonourable agreement. . . . The Court-Chancellor was of opinion that . . . it was quite possible to negotiate with the Elector just as other Princes and Republics had done, and by doing so get what we wanted; for the longer the German business lasts, the worse for us. If it does come to a breach [with Saxony], our own German troops will desert us. If our army consisted of French, Scots and

Swedes, we could no doubt put up a fight; but as it is, our army is entirely composed of Germans. Conscription at home is at the moment out of the question. The Chancellor [Oxenstierna], in his anxiety to escape humiliation, is firmly determined to die over there in Germany; but this will hardly do the country much good: we shall be forced to make peace just the same. The burden of defence will be intolerable in the long run; and in any case peace will have to be made sooner or later.

Ibid., 194-5

(*d*)

23 October. It was considered wisest and best to start a negotiation with the Emperor, and extricate ourselves from the German war: if it cannot be done on honourable terms, then let us content ourselves with whatever terms we can get; for the resources of the country are not adequate to the maintenance of great armies.

. . . .

The Court-Chancellor said also, that we wage war in Germany as auxiliaries, and not as principals. If the principals have now done a deal with the enemy, who can say that we are behaving dishonourably, if we cut ourselves off from the whole business?

Ibid., 222, 224

XXXVI The Problem of Disengagement

(*a*)

Resolution of the Regency and the Council of the Realm, concerning the continuing of peace-negotiations, and if need be of the war in Germany. 1 August 1636

Whereas the Chancellor upon his return has reported on the position in Germany at the time of his departure, and particularly on the negotiations for peace with the Emperor and the Elector of Saxony, which have been proceeding for almost a year, through the intermediary of Duke Adolf Frederick of Mecklenburg . . . ; the Regency and the Council have found these draft-terms reasonable, useful and honourable to the Queen and country. . . .

... We have given all these things our careful attention, and having entreated God, have now by His aid reached the following conclusions:

First, that we ought to pitch the terms of the sixth article (concerning restitution of the oppressed Protestant Electors, Prince and Estates) as high as is practicable; for (i) it is our Christian duty to take up their cause, and so try to preserve God's congregation in those places; (ii) it is conformable to the attitude and actions of our late King, who shed his blood for that cause; (iii) the safety of this country depends upon the liberties of the Estates in Germany not being transformed into a servitude, under the absolute domination of the House of Austria, and especially in keeping that House away from the Baltic; (iv) it is a question of honour, which in politics can never be ignored; (v) it gives us the goodwill and affection of all our neighbours, and of many Estates and soldiers in the Holy Roman Empire; (vi) and lastly, it seems unwise to give up this point before we are sure of the two others (the Crown's indemnity and the contentment of the soldiery), since if the first point were let go, either our adversary would seize the opportunity to evade the other two, or else if the negotiation broke down on them, all concerned would be alienated from us, and their jealousy of us would be even greater than before. For these and other reasons we have decided that this point must be stuck to as firmly as possible, and that we should aim at keeping the discussion of it going, while we press on in the meantime with ... the negotiation of the two other points. But since (1) the state of the country does not permit us to continue the war, unless it be unavoidably necessary; (2) the advantages of the war now fall to our neighbours, while the damage falls upon us; (3) the Evangelical Electors, Princes and Estates have not stood by us either constantly or sincerely: most of them have left the League [of Heilbronn], and (which is worse) attached themselves to the enemy; the most important of the rest are carrying on separate negotiations with him, and if there are still a few who are not, that is only because they have no hope of obtaining terms; (4) consequently we can expect no assistance from any state, but (5) have much more reason to fear that not only the German princes, but also foreign potentates may be induced to make common cause with our enemies. ... For these and other reasons, the Regency and Council do not consider it either reasonable or advisable that we should in the last resort persist with the war for the sake of others; but as soon as the two points of the Crown's indemnity and the contentment of the soldiery shall have been settled, then, when all reasonable means to aid the German Estates have been tried without success, we should drop the contentious article about the extent of the [Emperor's] amnesty and the restitution of the [German] Estates, and should leave it to the Estates themselves to deal with. Thereafter we should give them all possible assistance, not with the sword and under the hazards of war, but by intercession and other amicable means, and without prejudice to our own attempts to find an acceptable means of withdrawing from the war.

. . . .

Concerning the Crown's indemnity, we must insist that the treaty provide a considerable sum of money – up to 6 million *riksdaler* or more, if we are to abandon all lands and towns, though if need be we might accept 3 million *rdr*, together with the payment of the Crown's debts incurred here and there in Germany. But if the Crown were freed from all claims of the soldiery, as well as from its own outstanding debts in Germany, we might press for a sizeable cash payment, and thereby (since the situation of the German Estates is not such at present that they can find the money) keep possession of some of the harbours under the guise of security: the total sum might be abated by at the most a million *rdr*, and the main security should be in western Pomerania, Rügen, Kolberg and Wismar, and we should so arrange it that the garrisons be maintained without cost to the crown. Some concessions, as has been said, may well be made on this point of indemnity, and it is reasonable rather to give way than at this critical time to deprive the country of its gains, and commit it to a perpetual war, to the advantage of others and the hurt and danger of ourselves. But above all things we must try to obtain the contentment of the soldiery, and relieve Her Majesty and the crown of that burden, which should not and must not be placed upon her, since she receives no benefit from them, but rather hurt and extortion. Nevertheless since it would not be advisable nor honourable to the country to leave the soldiery entirely unsatisfied, the burden must be taken from our shoulders and transferred by agreement to those of the German Estates; and on this we must strictly insist.

As regards the ratification of the alliance with France, there is certainly something to be said for it, if in the end we are forced to go on fighting: but since it would bind our hands too tightly, and we should thereby be compelled to keep in the war even though an opportunity might arise to get out of it, it seems most advisable to defer the ratification as long as we can, on one pretext or another, till we see what happens to the Duke of Mecklenburg's negotiation. If it goes well, we had best cut loose from the war. If it sticks, we must ratify the alliance, and commend our cause to God.

Axel Oxenstiernas skrifter och brevvexling, I, i, 574–9

(*b*)

Oxenstierna on the French alliance, 1640

The Chancellor: I say, as I have always said, that there are many arguments to dissuade me from the French alliance. I have had experience of their tricks in former years. They commit hostile acts against us, under a mask of friendship. When we remonstrate with them about [taking] Breisach, and how they debauched the Army of [Bernard of] Weimar, they make long speeches, and trot out excuses, and shrug their shoulders. Our late King often tore his hair at the impertinences he had to put up with from them. But what could he do? Necessity is a great argument, and for a handful of gold one must often sacrifice reputation.

Svenska riksrådets protokoll, viii, 329

XXXVII Denmark and Germany, 1643

By 1643 Sweden's prospects had much improved. The renewal of the French subsidies had been followed by military successes, and already in 1641 the belligerents had agreed that there should be a peace congress at Münster and Osnabrück. But the attitude of Denmark gave rise to irritation and anxiety. Christian IV showed signs of trying to act as mediator, and the Swedes rightly supposed that this would not be to their advantage. His raising of the level of the Sound Tolls in 1638–9 annoyed the maritime powers: hence the conclusion of a Dutch-Swedish alliance in 1640. By the terms of the peace of Knäred (1613) Sweden's traditional exemption from the Sound Tolls had been reaffirmed; but Christian refused to extend this to Sweden's new possessions in Germany. In 1640 he had greatly annoyed the Swedish regency by assisting the clandestine departure of the Queen Mother to Denmark: Maria Eleonora had been on bad terms with the Regents since Gustav Adolf's death; she was a neurotic woman who had been excluded from the regency by Gustav Adolf himself, and she had not been permitted to supervise Christina's upbringing. The opportunity to scotch Danish plans and retort upon Danish provocations was to good to miss. Torstensson was ordered to attack Jutland from the south; the Dutch assisted Sweden; and the peace of Brömsebro brought Sweden (*inter alia*) Bremen and Verden, which had been in the possession of Prince

Frederick of Denmark. – Since the accession of the Great Elector in 1640, Sweden's relations with Brandenburg had taken a turn for the better; but the Swedish claim to Pomerania, as *satisfactio*, was still a bone of contention between them. The plan here put forward, of acquiring it as a forfeited pledge for an unpaid cash indemnity, proved to have no future. At Westphalia Sweden did indeed gain Western Pomerania, with Stettin, but only at the price of the Great Elector's lifelong hostility. And as to the 'contentment of the soldiery', Westphalia saw it whittled down to a mere 5 millions.

Resolution of the Council of the Realm on war with Denmark and conditions for peace in Germany, May 1643

. . . .

1. First. It is obvious, from the King of Denmark's public conduct and secret intrigues, that he is contemplating war against us. This appears from a variety of his recent actions; and particularly the provocation he has given us by his occupation of Pinneberg and the diocese of Bremen, . . . by his unreasonable treatment of Swedish denizens and subjects (and particularly merchants) at the Sound, and by his assisting the departure of Her Majesty's mother, the Queen Dowager, from this realm. And even though we were to suffer these things (and others like them) in patience, and postpone a reckoning to a more convenient time, there are now added to them such practices and enterprises as can neither be passed over nor postponed without the irremediable injury and certain destruction of the realm, since they openly proclaim that the determination to make war against us is already taken, and all they are working for now is to prepare a proper opportunity: as may be seen from their intrigues in Poland and Russia, and also from the way they treat us at the Sound, which is insufferable, and contrary to their agreements. For they now lay an excise on all imports of foreign liquor, and they arrest, unload and confiscate practically all Swedish ships and cargoes, under one pretext or another, so that scarcely anybody now may venture to avail himself of his right to sail the seas and trade freely; . . . and lastly their intentions are reflected in the innovations which they have introduced [in the tolls] at Ruden, in the recent Danish demonstration (undertaken without any imminent danger), when the King of Denmark put to sea with his entire fleet, and mobilized all his forces on land – either with a view to attacking us at home or abroad, or to intervene as a third party (as they say) and force us to accept such a settlement of the [German] war as may suit himself, and thereafter turn his arms against us. These are matters of such

importance that they must be considered in good time; and we must take counsel together how such misfortunes may (with God's help) be averted, and whether we have cause enough to justify a war? And if so, whether we ought to take the initiative against the enemy, or await his attack?

2. Next, assuming that we have full and satisfactory grounds for waging a just war, what steps we can take to avoid it, so that the country does not become involved in hostilities at an untimely moment; or, if we do become involved in them, how the war is to be conducted?

3. Since the peace-negotiations [at Westphalia] have been generally agreed upon, and the day fixed upon which the congress is to meet, it is necessary to discuss what indemnity is to be proposed, and what insisted on; in which connexion we must make up our minds whether it will be advisable to demand and insist upon Pomerania, or whether it would not be better to consider some other satisfaction, so that our diplomats and soldiers may shape their conduct accordingly.

All these matters having been fully canvassed in the course of the last few days, and argument heard for and against, in the light of such reports as have come to hand and such information as could be elicited, we have at length decided and resolved as follows:

I

First. That it is the King of Denmark's intention to hurt, hinder, belittle and bring into contempt Her Majesty and the crown of Sweden, wherever and whenever he can; to incite one enemy after another against us; to distract our forces as much as possible; and to stir up trouble in the country as he shall find opportunity. Against these things we must take counter-measures in good time, suffering some of them in patience, and avoiding a conflict (as hitherto) as long as it is a question only of plans and intentions, rather than of overt acts. But now that projects are turning into realities, it is no longer possible to sit still in cover, or try to gain time: we must either oppose a timely resistance, and look to the country's interests, or expect to be overwhelmed by a sudden attack. . . . And therefore the lords of the Council find that the grounds and reasons for war with Denmark are sound, strong and satisfactory; and that we may begin hostilities with a good conscience, as being a righteous war; . . . so that if the King of Denmark continue taking toll, confiscating, interrupting navigation in the Sound, and other such proceedings, and is not to be moved from that course of action, then our best course would be to begin the war (as well now as later!) and rather throw its burdens upon him, than sit waiting to be attacked by him at home.

II

Next, it seems necessary and prudent to make an attempt to smooth out the disputes with Denmark by trying the means which are provided by treaty, and have been usual in the past. . . . It would not be a bad thing, either, to seek an opportunity to revive our old friendship with the Tsar by sending an embassy to him, and thus as far as possible forestall any Danish plots and take the edge off any controversies that may arise. It is particularly necessary to get in touch with Field-Marshal Lindorm [*sic*: *sc.* Lennart] Torstensson, and put him in the picture about the whole situation, and our policy in regard to it; and to order him to give the highest priority to keeping his army in such a state that he may be able to move to the coast in the autumn, either through the Mark of Brandenburg or on the other side of the Elbe through Lüneburg territory, as he may find most convenient, so that when the Danish forces withdraw he may be able to follow them and take up his winter quarters in Holstein and Jutland. . . . In the meantime, while all this is being quietly and secretly arranged, it might be as well to give advance notice to some of the leading Estates, confidentially inform them of the position, and get their approval, by way of additional security in case things should turn out ill: this has been usual in the past, and was always done by His late Majesty in important matters which involved serious consequences. And since we concluded an alliance with the States-General of the Netherlands three years ago for no other purpose than to safeguard trade and navigation in the Baltic and North Seas, and in the Sound, they too should be written to, their assistance should be sought, and they should be stimulated to make the alliance effective by coöperating with us. Private merchants and shippers in Holland should also be induced to help us, either with money, or by such other evidences of good-will as may be most convenient. . . .

III

Concerning the indemnity for the crown of Sweden, . . . and the terms which we must formulate and insist on in the peace negotiations, it seems very clear that this was the real reason why the King of Denmark put himself forward as mediator; his idea being that he could put obstacles in the way of our gaining anything that would be convenient or useful to us, and also obtain some advantages for himself. It is also the case that this question of indemnity has deterred many from seeking our friendship, and particularly the Elector of Brandenburg, who is afraid that we may seek our satisfaction in Pomerania. And this is not less a matter of concern to the King of Denmark – indeed, it is the thing which he finds hardest to swallow; it made him arm this year; it provoked the lively correspondence between Denmark and Poland. Since Pomerania is such a thorn in the flesh both to our neighbours and to many others, and arouses such jealousy against us, we have hitherto claimed indemnity in general terms, and neither specified nor pressed for Pomerania. But if the thing be soberly considered, there is certainly no solution more convenient, more practicable and more honourable for the Holy Roman Empire than to allow the Swedish crown to keep Pomerania as satisfaction for war expenses, to recognize the crown as holding an imperial fief, in the same way as the King of Denmark holds Holstein, and to allow the crown a vote in the Upper Saxon Circle, at the Imperial Diet and at all other meetings of the Estates. We should be permitted to retain the Pomeranian ports in order to secure the Baltic coast against the House of Austria, and other ill-disposed powers; with full freedom to raise mercenaries, and to refuse this privilege to our neighbours. It would give us the possibility of always being able to keep an eye on our neighbours at close range, and in time of war we should be in a position to take them in the rear. There are many such reasons; and they apply equally to Wismar. But when we consider all the opposition which the proposal will arouse, and the counter-mines which Poland and Denmark are preparing, and will prepare; the great difficulty of bringing the Emperor to assent to it; and the antagonistic reaction it will produce in the Elector of Brandenburg (now, after the extinction of the ducal house of Pomerania, the guaranteed successor) – there is no doubt that while we may certainly propose Pomerania as our indemnity we shall not get it unless we are prepared to go on fighting for it; and it is easy to envisage what difficulties that might land us in, especially if the peace negotiations were to break down on that point only. All this is to say nothing of the fact that even in peace-time Pomerania can be held only if it is given strong garrisons; for the towns and Estates of Pomerania dislike Swedish rule, and malevolent neighbours will always have designs on it, especially at times when the Swedish crown may happen to be in difficulties, either at home or with some neighbour. So that if one looks squarely at the problem, it is clear that satisfaction in Pomerania is not obtainable by negotiation, but is bound to provoke all sorts of cabals and conspiracies against us in one place or another; and therefore it would be wisest not to incur the odium of it, especially since there are few powers who look with any favour on the demand for satisfaction, even when framed in general terms, and still fewer, when it is particularized. If we pitch on some other territory, the same objections will apply, and someone else will have to pay the price, wherever we choose; to say nothing of the fact that no other territory lies so conveniently for Sweden. It seems therefore that the most practicable line is not directly to declare our views on Pomerania, but to press as strongly as possible for the payment of the army's arrears, either in money or in land, without specifying where; and if they choose to pay in money, to ask then that Pomerania and Wismar be handed over as security, and that the terms of payment, and the instalments, be carefully laid down; and if these terms are not complied with, that the securities fall to the crown in perpetual possession. . . . This, it seems, might be proposed with some show of reason, and without arousing the jealousy of any interested party; and in such a case it might be possible to reach agreement in advance with the Elector of Brandenburg (as the party principally concerned) and by playing on his hope of acquiring Pomerania induce him to coöperate in the peace-negotiations, and in the contentment of the soldiery, or at the very least keep him in play so that he did not actually enter into an alliance with Denmark and Poland against us. . . .

The amount of money which might reasonably be asked, and should be asked, for our expenses, might first be fixed at 2 million *rdr* for every year of the war, which makes 26 millions, since the war is now in its 13th year; but this might be gradually cut down to a million a year, or 13 millions in all. And if the contentment of the soldiery be deducted from that, this seems not unreasonable. If we estimate the soldier's arrears at from 1 to 5 millions, and the [German] Estates undertook to pay it, the crown would receive (over and above demands of the army) some 8 or at the absolute minimum 6 millions, and besides that would hold in pawn either the whole of Pomerania, or Western Pomerania, Wismar and certain dependent territories.

These are to be declared to be the minimum terms upon which Her Majesty will be satisfied, and it is to be presumed that nobody can reasonably object to them if the crown can be induced to part with the territorial advantages now in its hands. [Better terms should, however, be obtained if at all possible.] These are the ultimate and final proposals for indemnity; and the members of the Council do not support them as good in themselves, but because seeing the great dangers which threaten the country if the war goes on, as well as others which seem probable, they think such terms preferable to a continuance of hostilities. . . .

Axel Oxenstiernas skrifter och brevvexling, I, i, 580–7

XXXVIII Christina and the Negotiations at Westphalia, 1647

Christina's views on foreign policy tended to be shaped by personal rather than national considerations. She had begun to find the prestige and authority of Axel Oxenstierna irksome; she may have been taught to suspect the ambitions of the Oxenstierna family: at all events, she was now sympathizing with Oxenstierna's political enemies, and particularly with men like Johan Adler Salvius. Salvius and Johan Oxenstierna were the Swedish delegates to Westphalia. They were on the worst of terms personally, and at odds politically, Salvius being for securing peace by concessions, Oxenstierna for standing out for better terms. Hence for the moment Christina was for peace too; though with typical frivolity she was prepared to jeopardize the negotiation in order to secure Benfeld for her favourite Magnus Gabriel de la Gardie. It flattered her vanity to be Queen of a victorious nation of resurgent Goths; but to be hailed as the pacificator of Europe would flatter it no less.

(*a*)

Queen Christina to Johan Oxenstierna and Johan Adler Salvius, 10 April [1647]

Gentlemen,

I add these few words in my own hand to my official letter, in order to discover to you my alarm lest the peace negotiations, which until this moment have borne so favourable an aspect, should be blocked; and this for reasons of which I am totally ignorant. And that you may be in no uncertainty as to my wishes, [this is to inform you that] you may certainly take it for granted that I desire above all things a safe and honourable peace. And since the question of our indemnity has already been disposed of, and the only matters still to be arranged are the contentment of the soldiery and the grievances of the States of the Empire, it is my will that you keep the negotiations going on an amicable footing, until Erskine has arrived and acquainted you with the nature of his commission; after which you will without delay bring the negotiation to a satisfactory conclusion: for the [German] States, and in the matter of our indemnity and the contentment of the soldiery, you will obtain the best terms that are to be had without risk of a rupture; and you will refrain from protracting the negotiations, as you have done in the past. And if you fail in this, you may look to it how you will answer for it to God, to the Estates of the Realm, and to Me. If it is a matter of concern to you to escape my severest displeasure, if you have no ambition to answer for your conduct in my presence, and be forced to stand before me with a countenance alternating between white and red, you will take care not to allow yourselves to be deflected from your object by the imaginings of ambitious men. For you may be perfectly assured that neither personal eminence, nor aristocratic backing, will deter me from manifesting to the whole world the displeasure with which I view unreasonable proceedings. For I am very sure that if it went ill with the treaty I should find myself, by your fault, involved in a labyrinth from which neither you, nor those whose intrigues were responsible, would be very likely to extricate me. You will do well, then, to have a care what you do. I have no doubt that you will; and I write this simply for your information, having such full reliance upon your discretion that I confidently expect (with God's help) a successful outcome to these long-drawn negotiations. And if in these matters you continue to give evidence of your fidelity, you may rest assured that upon your return you will find me always your well-affectioned

Christina.

(*b*)

Queen Christina to Johan Adler Salvius, 10 April 1647

Your various letters have given me a clear idea of the present state of the peace-negotiations; and I see very plainly how hard you have been working to put an end to the long and bloody war which for so many years has afflicted the whole of Europe. But I also deduce from all this that there are those who are doing their best to spin out the discussions, if not indeed to wreck the treaty altogether. I shall not fail to reward your zeal and fidelity. As to the other party, I intend to act in such a way that the whole world will know that the fault does not lie with me; and I shall let them see that not even the R.C. [Rikscantzler: Axel Oxenstierna] can move the world with his little finger. . . . The letter which accompanies this [(*a*), above] is directed to both of you, and you are to deliver it to G[reve] J[ohan] O[xenstierna]: although I say harsh things about you in it, they are not meant to apply to you, but to him only. Contrive that d'Avaux is made aware of the contents, so that they may know where the fault lies: I should not like them to get wrong ideas about me. I am sending Erskine to you to let you know more at large about the contentment of the soldiery: I have done as much as I could about this, and do not doubt that you will continue to do everything possible to help on the negotiation: you may be entirely assured that I will support you on this question, and when at last God sends you home with a peace, I will reward your services by appointing you to the Council of the Realm, which as you know is the highest honour to which any Swede may aspire; and if there were any higher degree of honour, I would not hesitate to confer it on you. But it will not be done, I fancy, without arousing a good deal of ill-feeling. . . . For the rest, I trust you to press on with the negotiations with the same admirable fidelity which you have always shown upon all occasions. Try above all to keep the French in a good opinion of me, so that the dislike of that nation shown by a certain party [Johan Oxenstierna] does not redound to my hurt. I hope my actions will make it clear what my real sentiments are.

I recommend to you the interests of Count Magnus [de la Gardie], as though they were my own. If you could give me a hint or a suggestion as to how I could confer Benfeld upon him, or some other considerable territory, I should be only too pleased. I would much like to give him Benfeld, but I hesitate to do so until I know your opinion. Keep this to yourself at all costs, until I can find out whether it can be done. . . . But speak to M. d'Avaux about it. I flatter myself that he is too courteous to make any difficulty about doing so considerable a service to one of his most affectionate friends and servants; or rather, I think he would not take it amiss if I were to say to him that by working for a friend of mine (and thereby making him a friend of *his*) he would give me one of the most signal marks of affection that I ever solicited of him. I beg you, then, to assure M. d'Avaux of the esteem I have for his person; tell him that the private services he has rendered me are so considerable that I should be mortally disappointed if I were deprived of the hope of repaying at least a part of what he has done for me.

With this I close. God keep you. Take care that the roan doesn't kick over the traces! I am your always well-affectioned

Christine.

Do let me know what sort of a face G.J.O. makes when he reads my letter to you both.

Arckenholtz, *Mémoires concernant Christine, Reine de Suède*, i, 110-11, 112-15

XXXIX Karl X Gustav and the Eastern Crisis, 1654

The crisis in Poland which followed Chmielnicki's revolt, and the Russian intervention which flowed from it, faced Sweden with the possibility that Poland might disintegrate, and Russia acquire the remaining Polish coastlands. Some precautionary measures on Sweden's side were therefore justified. But by this time it was becoming clear that Sweden could not keep a large army embodied unless its pay and maintenance could be provided at the expense of enemy territory: if troops were raised, they must be used; mobilization entailed war. The older view of Swedish policy saw Denmark as the natural enemy, and had grown used to friendship with Russia; Karl Gustav, on the other hand, saw Russia as Sweden's most dangerous potential rival. He also saw the solution to the financial problem in the recovery of the Prussian tolls, lost in 1635. All attempts to obtain a peace (as against a truce) with Poland had failed, and the Polish Vasas still disputed the claims of the Swedish junior line. Karl Gustav therefore determined to forestall the Russians and secure Prussia. The risk that Denmark might seek revenge for Brömsebro was never forgotten; but for the moment that problem could wait. The debates printed below vividly illustrate the Swedish dilemma: note how even the champions of peace and economy, by accepting the need for mobilization, in effect throw in their hands.

Minutes of the Council of the Realm, 8-12 December 1654

The Chancellor [Erik Oxenstierna]: . . . The Proposition is not that we should make war on this country or that. But we have resolved once already to mobilize, and indeed in present circumstances it is inevitable. The question now is whom to keep our eye on; where the greatest danger seems to lie; and where we can best safeguard our interests.

The Steward [Per Brahe]: If we raise six or seven German regiments, besides our own militia – and we could scarcely do with less – and then leave them unoccupied, it will be as good as making war upon ourselves: think how much will have been wasted on maintaining them!

Herr Bengt Skytte sought to show that the danger from Russia was not as yet very great. . . .

. . . .

The Chancellor: We are not at this stage thinking about making war on anybody; but we have resolved that the danger is such that we ought to arm. Hitherto we have been discussing, in quite general terms, the morality and utility of war; now we must determine the particular point: against whom we are mobilizing, and where the greatest danger lies. . . .

Herr Christer Bonde: As to Denmark, 1. it may be true that they are not arming, but all the same they are steadily building up their navy, and it is already quite formidable; 2. the agreement between Denmark, Poland and the Dutch to arm their ships in the Baltic looks suspicious; 3. the alliance between Holland and Denmark is directed against us. Denmark is jealous of us because we possess almost all the harbours in the Baltic, and hence her Sound Tolls are diminished, not to mention the fact that by trading ourselves we exclude the commerce of other nations who would have paid toll. The Dutch are jealous of our power, and because our trade is increasing. . . .

The Chancellor: There is something in that; but we have in fact no information that Denmark is concerting measures with Poland or the Dutch to arm in the Baltic. The King of Denmark's interest, like ours, is to keep all foreign warships *out* of the Baltic.

The Steward: You can't blame the Danes for wanting to build up their fleet. We shall always be capable of dealing with them, and there seems no immediate danger from that quarter. Holland has been weakened by England, and by internal dissension. . . . But Denmark lies as it were between Germany, Holland and England, and none of these would wish to see her ruined. Denmark has many friends in the Empire. . . . The case would be altered, of course, if Denmark were attacked by some other power, and its destruction seemed imminent: in that case we might do well to grab a bit for ourselves, like everybody else. . . . Poland seems to be in danger of that kind at this moment.

. . . .

Count Gustav Leijonhufvud moved that it be war. And suggested that if nobody should start a war against us, we should attack the Russians.

The Chancellor: We are discussing mobilization, not war.

The Treasurer [Magnus Gabriel de la Gardie]: We must direct our thoughts to the quarter where the danger is greatest, and it is argued that it is greatest on the side of Russia. . . .

. . . .

The Chancellor: . . . I take it that we are all agreed to adhere to the proposal that we should arm; that we do it with a view to the war between Poland and Russia; and that it is in this quarter that the troops are to be employed.

To this all members of the Council assented.

The Chancellor then continued with the second question, namely whether the mobilization was to be considered as simply designed for the defence of our own fortresses, or for a campaign in the field? . . .

The Steward. I am afraid that it begins to look as though Poland is too weak to resist the Russian attack for long. And it is a matter of concern to us that Poland shall not fall wholly into the hands of the Muscovites. It might not be a bad thing to avail ourselves of their predicament, and tell them plainly that there are unsettled controversies between us, and say 'you have done this and this contrary to the armistice agreement; now you are heavily involved with the Russians, which is a thing we are interested in ourselves; and you must just agree to a reasonable settlement with us, or be prepared for our taking our cut, just as the Russians do'. If it comes to a settlement . . . we could on certain terms agree to come to Poland's rescue; but if it doesn't, it would be best to take the chance and use our opportunity. In this way we could either help her or skelp her, according to how she behaved. . . .

Herr Christer Bonde reminded them that there are only five years of the truce [of Stuhmsdorf] to run, and what is to prevent us tackling the question now, just as well as a few years later, when perhaps we should not have such an opportunity? . . .

The Chancellor: This is the best moment for the country to get a proper settlement of our disputes with Poland. But what means are we to use for this purpose? . . . His Excellency thought, for his part, that we must say flat out: either you reach an agreement with us at once, or you will get what's coming to you.

The Steward reminded them what a heavy burden it would be if they were to arm, and then sit down and do nothing. . . . It would be well for both of us – Poland and ourselves – that there should be negotiations this winter. . . . And we could bargain with them on the basis that if agreement were reached now, we would help them against the Russians. But if it should prove impossible to get anywhere with the Poles by peaceful negotiation, His Excellency felt that the best and most prudent course would be to make use of this good opportunity to obtain the maximum advantage from them as well as from the Russians. He asked them to reflect how deplorable it would be to allow such a chance to slip through their fingers, and also how profitable our wars have been to us. And now our armies are ageing, our generals are getting old and dropping off; and we know, from the scantiness of our resources, and the warlike temper of our nation, what it was that prompted the expeditions of the ancient Goths to other lands. Such reasons as these – if the cause were good – are arguments enough for arming.

11 December, 1654. [The debate resumed: *The Chancellor* recapitulates:]

The Chancellor: We are discussing only the question of arming; and not the question of war. . . . And to keep within the limits of our discussion, I suggest that we have to ask ourselves two questions: 1. Whether we shall advise H.M. to arm, or whether we think that we shall be able to go on remaining at peace, if we do not arm; 2. Assuming that we advise mobilization, where are the troops to be employed?

. . . .

The Steward observed . . . that one of two things could happen: either that Poland and Muscovy became reconciled and joined forces to attack us; or that Poland might succumb entirely. This implies that we must be prepared. . . . It would certainly be a good thing to dispose of Denmark once for all. But at the moment it does not seem that there is much risk from that quarter, nor could His Excellency see any just cause of war. . . . As to the situation on the other side, it is likely that an accomodation could be reached with Poland, but it might be more difficult with the Tsar. The pretensions which he advances against Poland are pretensions which he also advances against us. . . .

. . . .

Herr Christer Bonde: . . . It certainly seems reasonable to turn to the quarter where the immediate danger seems greatest, but the execution of such a policy would not be without difficulties. For as soon as we engaged ourselves against Poland, Denmark and Holland would join forces against us. These powers would be jealous of our tolls at Pillau. And he reminded them again of the difficulties which had been caused by these tolls in the last war.

. . . .

The Steward thought we ought not to look so hard at the lesser danger that we lost sight of the greater and more serious one. We had to bear all these considerations in mind during the last war with Poland, but the late King did not allow them to stop him, and in the end he did effect a reconciliation with Denmark, in the year 1624. We must have some respect for our pledged word. . . . And in any case we should not suppose that it is so easy to attack and conquer another crown and country, especially in view of the King of Denmark's alliances, his fortresses, his resources in manpower, his geographical situation. . . . We are so placed, behind forests and skerries, that no enemy will find it very easy to attack us. The toll will no doubt exasperate the Dutch, but it can't be helped; it has happened before, and they would have to put up with it, now as then.

The Chancellor: If we compare the two possible sources of danger at the moment, it is clear that on the one hand we have neighbours already armed, and the flames of war are already on our frontiers. We know that they have hostile intentions towards us. And we have plenty of grievances against them. On the side of Denmark all this may possibly be the case; on the other side it *is* the case already. . . . We have always good reasons available for a war against Denmark; but not always such good ones as at present on the other front. . . . It would be a simple matter afterwards to start a war with Denmark; but such a war would not be without considerable difficulties. We know what a job we had with Denmark last time, when we had Holland on our side; and how would it be now?

. . . .

Herr Herman Fleming: . . . When we look at the country's finances . . . the wisest thing is to avoid war if we possibly can. We must indeed keep an eye on Denmark. But it would be best, in the first instance, to see if we cannot avoid all large commitments. I do not think, therefore, that we should attack the Russians because of the situation in Poland.

The Chancellor: There has certainly never been any question of attacking anybody; it is a question only of arming.

Herr Herman Fleming: Yes, I approve of arming, provided that we negotiate behind the scenes.

Herr Bengt Skytte advised that we make every effort to secure peace, and give no cause or occasion for a rupture; but entirely agreed with other members that we should counsel H.M., in view of the dangers of the present moment, to provide himself with a considerable force....

. . . . . .

[The Chancellor then summed up the day's debate. They were agreed that they would advise a considerable armament; and its prime object was defined as security against Poland.]

12 December 1654

The Chancellor: [The King wishes the following point to be put to the Council.] Since mobilization is unavoidable, and H.M. must therefore reinforce his native troops with mercenary forces, what is to happen if Poland, after we have mobilized, should give way on our two main points [i.e. abandon their claims to Livonia, and to the Swedish crown]? Should we accept that, and start paying off the troops at once; or would it be better – and indeed, would not our outlay on arming demand – that we screw up our terms, and try to get something which would both satisfy the wage-claims of the mercenaries, and provide security that Poland would make no more trouble? ... [He is in favour of the latter] both as being safer in itself, and also because there is always the chance that other powers may get possession of what we have our eye on, and thus give us worse neighbours even than Poland. And there is also to be considered the point about paying the soldiery. For (1) otherwise the crown would have to pay them itself, which would be hard; (2) if the foreign officers were disbanded without having been in action, they might well be discontented, and feel that they had been made fools of....

. . . .

Count Carl Leijonhufvud [agreed with the Chancellor]. It is in any case out of the question that we can assemble any really imposing army without recruiting foreign mercenaries....

. . . .

Herr Bengt Skytte was of opinion that it would be well to get some security, and now was the time to get it; and mentioned Prussia, and discoursed on its usefulness to Sweden. 1. Prussia is the eye of the

Baltic; 2. a bastion for Livonia; 3. so situated that it can hold Poland and Brandenburg in check. . . . Was in favour of full mobilization, both of native troops and foreign mercenaries . . . and that it was advisable to make the best use of our chances, and insist on the two main points of a solid security, and the contentment of the soldiery. . . . For the former, suggested the [Prussian] coast. And considered it would be wisest if we extended our protection to all who asked for it, even if it should be to the whole of Poland.

. . . .

Herr Gustav Bonde: To insist on security and satisfaction, and to take others into our protection, is neither more nor less than to embark upon a new war; and we can't decide on that without the knowledge of the Estates. . . . If the most we can get from the King of Poland by way of concession is the abandonment of his claims on the Swedish crown, and on Livonia, we had better be content with that, and then, uniting our forces with Poland, turn against Russia, which is now the most formidable power, and the one which needs watching. What would the prospect be, if Poland were reconciled with the Muscovite, and they joined hands to attack us!

The Chancellor: But what about the contentment of the soldiery?

Herr Gustav Bonde: We should just have to try to get the best terms we can from Poland, using such opportunities as might present themselves.

The Chancellor: . . . There may be danger in delay. The Russians may perhaps invade Kurland.

[He sums up the sense of the meetings: full armament; Sweden to insist that Poland gives real security, and satisfies the mercenaries, besides abandoning claims to Sweden and Livonia; protection to be offered to all who ask for it. And he continues:]

All this does not amount to advising the beginning of a new war, for the consent of the Estates is necessary for that; but it proceeds from a determination to ward off dangers in time, and from a due care for H.M.'s interests. . . .

Svenska riksrådets protokoll, xvi, 3-36

XL Karl Gustav's designs on Denmark, 1658

After Karl Gustav's victory over Denmark early in 1658 he had two main objects: to make peace with his remaining enemies, and to secure the Prussian tolls. He hoped that Austria would induce the Poles to make a peace which would leave Prussia in his hands; failing that, he was prepared to partition Poland either with Austria or with Russia. But if no peace could be had, or if its conclusion seemed likely to be a lengthy business, he must somehow support his armies in the meantime: a war against Austria, or even against Brandenburg (who coveted Swedish Pomerania) might provide the means. By June, however, he was turning to the idea of war against Denmark. If he could conquer Denmark and annex the Sound Tolls his financial problems would be solved without the conquest of Prussia, and the old Swedish dream of controlling trade between Russia and the West might be realized. Denmark's tardiness and evasiveness in complying with the Roskilde peace-terms gave him a pretext. He therefore abandoned the Prussian project and concentrated on Denmark. The severity of the settlement he envisaged in these discussions was even exceeded in his conversations with the French ambassador, Terlon, to whom he spoke of imprisoning the Danish royal family, and razing Copenhagen.

Minutes of meetings of [an itinerant section of] the Council of the Realm

7 July 1658. Gottorp

H.M. talked of Thorn, and how it has been attacked by the Poles. And that it was not reasonable to relax our grip on the Danish business in so uncertain a situation. Nor was it advisable to concentrate on securing Thorn, if it should seem to be better to take some other place from the Elector [of Brandenburg] instead. To remain in the area and do nothing was not to be recommended either. If H.M. were to be prevented from relieving Thorn, and *as a result of Denmark's temporizing were to lose it*, H.M. would have *good reason to indemnify himself at the expense of Denmark*. H.M. asked what the Council thought about it, since it would be hurtful to us to continue inactive; time was passing; and soon the troops would start to desert.

Herr Gustav Baner thought that if H.M. were to attack Denmark again, he had good grounds for it.

Count Tott was of the same opinion. The King of Denmark had shown no good-will in carrying out the peace terms.

. . . .

Count Wrangel thought that we should wait for a reply from Denmark.

H.M. answered that they had dragged out the whole business as long as possible, and he did not know whether we could expect anything further from them. . . . H.M. asked the Council's views on this proposal: whether, in the event of their having reached no settlement in Copenhagen ... H.M. might not launch an attack on Denmark? *Resolved, that this should be done; and unless a settlement has already been reached the Commissioners are not to conclude one, but H.M. will then make his preparations for war.* Notification of this to be sent at once to the Commissioners.

23 July 1658. Wismar

H.M. discussed the disinclination of the Austrians to make peace, and the multiplicity of our other enemies. And that it seemed *a bad thing to involve oneself in the long-drawn business of negotiation before being certain of Denmark, since it would give the appearance of irresoluteness.* Denmark's tergiversations in [carrying out the terms of the peace of Roskilde]....

Count Carl [*Leijonhufvud*]: Since H.M. has many enemies, and no security in his rear; and since it would be unwise to lose the advantage he has at present ... his humble opinion was that H.M. should make sure of Denmark, according to the resolution already taken.

. . . .

Count Jakob de la Gardie agreed with *Count Carl*, and was unreservedly of opinion that the resolution was wise and judicious.

H.M. asserted, on his conscience, that *until he was actually upon the march, and had observed Denmark's insidious intrigues,* he had not intended to take any such resolution.

H.M. discoursed on the affairs of Poland; said he saw that it was necessary by some means or other to have peace with them ... the most difficult thing was, how to get a congress arranged. That if H.M. makes any concessions to Poland, then Poland must separate from H.M.'s enemies Austria and Brandenburg. Pomerania must be safeguarded: for this 6000 men would be required. Where was the money for them to come from? ... H.M. could make no peace with Brandenburg unless at the same time he made it also with Austria.

. . . .

H.M. asked the opinion of the Council whether he should himself personally take part in the enterprise.... *Item*, whether, if God gave us good fortune, Denmark should not be reduced to the position of a province of Sweden? *Item*, whether the nobility there should be granted the same conditions as other Swedish subjects, or whether they should emigrate, being allowed to keep a fourth part of their property, the remainder being retained by H.M. or by him granted to others.

The nobility would never be faithful to H.M.; therefore let them emigrate.

Zealand, Falster and Laland might form one province, Jutland another, Fyn another, Two [*sic*] Supreme Courts, one in Zealand, one in Jutland, one in Norway.

H.M. would receive the oaths of allegiance in Skåne, and the Danes would have to come over there to take it. As to ceremonial, the Danish crown to be placed on a separate table, lower than the other. And H.M. would wear the Swedish.

As to laws, means could be found to let them have their own law, in so far as it was not repugnant to the fundamental law of the kingdom.

But the Form of Government to be as in Sweden.

They should be deprived of their university, which should be moved to Göteborg. Bishops who will not swear allegiance can emigrate, and Swedes be put in their places.

If there is any exchange of properties between the crown and the Danish nobility, they should be given land in Ingria, by way of colonizing that province.

Probably only the nobility will be against H.M., the other Estates not, since they will acquire status as free men, which they did not have before. Therefore the nobility must either emigrate [voluntarily], or H.M. must force them to go: middle courses are of no use here.

To coerce the nobility into emigration, hard conditions could be imposed upon them; such as putting them under overlords who would have jurisdiction, or putting Counts or Barons over them; which they would not easily suffer, but would prefer to emigrate. A good addition to these conditions would be if H.M. gave the Counts and Barons a feudal superiority over them, as in Germany. Those who openly oppose H.M.'s plans can be declared to have forfeited their estates without any conditions.

Not to be any great officers of government there.

Svenska riksrådets protokoll, xviii, 83–8

XLI Gustaf Bonde on the need for peace, 1661

In the generation after 1660 it was extraordinarily difficult for Swedish statesmen to devise a satisfactory foreign policy. Sweden was in theory still a great power, one of the guarantors of the Westphalian settlement; but it was unlikely that she could find the money for armies large enough to make her guarantee good. Like most Swedish statesmen of the sixties, Gustaf Bonde (cf. the note to **XXVIII**) recognized that the country must have peace, and could no longer behave as the equal of Louis XIV's France. The best hope was perhaps to keep up an appearance of great-power status by holding the balance between Habsburg and Bourbon, England and the Dutch, and if all went well to collect the prestige which attached to the part of mediator. But if the country could not afford a war, neither could it maintain from its own resources an army strong enough to ensure respect for its neutrality, and to lend weight to its mediation. Sweden, in short, could not afford to be either a neutral or a belligerent. There were only two ways out of this dilemma: one involved a rigorous Reduction; the other lay in inducing some foreign power – *any* foreign power, it hardly mattered which – to pay Sweden subsidies in peacetime. The Regents much preferred the second alternative; and in the twenty years after Karl Gustav's death Sweden became (what she was to be again after 1720) a subsidy-hunting power. It was a policy which entailed humiliations not easy to reconcile with the Regents' professed desire to make reputation and prestige a substitute for military glory. Nevertheless, until the outbreak of war in 1675 Sweden saved her face and concealed the truth well enough to deceive even experienced diplomats.

It is clear that war makes the most serious inroads upon the resources of the crown, and entails the impoverishment and ruin of the subject; and we have learned by experience that no war in past times has brought renown, profit or advantage to King and country, without also exacting large annual expenditure of our resources, and burdening the subject with taxes and conscriptions . . . , so that when our gains are measured against our sacrifices, they appear sufficiently dearly bought. It seems therefore necessary that we make up our minds to a period of peace, and lay aside all thought of war as long as peace is to be had. . . . By these means we can put ourselves in such a posture, at sea and on land, that should a war be forced upon us we shall be capable of accepting the challenge and emerging honourably from the contest. No doubt there are many arguments which might be advanced on the other side, and in particular the argument that war is more profitable to our nation than peace; for the wars of the last few years have had so fortunate an issue that the country has acquired high renown, rich provinces have been annexed, our army and our aristocracy have been exercised, employed and trained for service, so that a nobleman can live as befits his condition, rather than starve miserably at home, or take to other and less legitimate courses; and much more to the same purpose, in all of which there is a considerable element of truth. Nevertheless, it does not seem to be a good thing that we should flatter ourselves on the basis of the happy issue of these wars; nor is it wise to conclude that God has aided our righteous cause, and on that assumption direct our thoughts to further wars, and make plans upon the supposition that God will always arrange for a similar outcome to all our actions. We should remember rather that the issue of war is always uncertain, and is frequently most disastrous for those who believe themselves to have the justest cause for arming; what then may we not expect if out of mere ambition, and presuming upon our valour and every favour of fortune, we refuse to acquiesce in the conditions of a just peace, but rather use it as a basis for molesting others, and so hazard ourselves and our country, making ourselves odious to other nations, so that they are forced to band together for our defeat and destruction, as happened in recent years? If we care to compare other kingdoms and republics who have enjoyed the blessings of peace, we shall see how they progress and prosper, while those who are burdened with wars are so exhausted, that they may be said to be at death's door. . . . It seems wisest, therefore, for as long as our neighbours will allow it, to follow His late Majesty's injunction on his death-bed, and strive to keep the peace; and under the protection of peace to seek to put the country into a condition in which it is capable of fighting in a just cause, if an enemy should at last insist on disturbing our tranquillity. And for that we must have a care of our armed forces on sea and land – which we can hardly do, if we have no money to pay for them.

Printed (with commentary by Georg Wittrock) in *Historisk Tidskrift*, xxxiii (1913), pp. 45–6

XLII Magnus Gabriel de la Gardie's defence of his foreign policy, 1678

In the mid-seventies the inherent difficulties of Sweden's international position produced a catastrophe, and de la Gardie provided a convenient scapegoat. He had made the French alliance of 1672 because the gathering European crisis drove him to seek security by armaments for which the crown could no longer pay: hence foreign subsidies were essential. His aim was to keep the peace, preserve the European balance, build up a block of neutral states, and put Sweden in a position in which she could come forward as mediator and (in her capacity as guarantor of Westphalia) perhaps as arbiter too: hence the congress at Cologne in 1673, when Sweden vainly offered mediation to the belligerents. He did not realize that France might feel that it was not for services such as these that she was paying subsidies. In July 1674 he was made to realize it. In return for promises of large payments, Sweden had agreed to send considerable forces to Swedish Pomerania: de la Gardie intended them only to lend weight to his pacific policy; but France upset all his calculations by withholding most of the money until the Swedish troops actually began fighting. In a desperate effort to finance them, and still keep out of the war, de la Gardie was even willing to take subsidies simultaneously from the Dutch; but the Dutch declined the suggestion, and in September de la Gardie had to promise France that they should begin operations within six weeks of the landing of their commander, Wrangel. Even then he tried to avoid the commitment; but delays, confused and contradictory orders, and the urgent need to quarter the troops on foreign soil, led to Wrangel's violation of Brandenburg territory in December. The insignificant reverse of Fehrbellin followed in June: its consequences were disastrous because it led to declarations of war by the Dutch, the Empire, and (in September) Denmark. De la Gardie's defence of his policy contains much that is true; but it ignores the essential point that a country which is dependent on subsidies for bare security is in no position to have a foreign policy, however estimable its objectives.

Vindiciae veritatis; or, the defence of Truth against evil, cunning and lying accusations. Höjentorp, 1 February 1678

... Thus the reasons for the conclusion of the [French] alliance were these. *First*, to prevent England and France, out of dissatisfaction with Sweden, from turning to Denmark, and enlisting her in the war; for Sweden perceived that Denmark was ready to take every conceivable opportunity to engage in a war, in order to increase her importance; which she could not hope to do of her own resources, but only by contracting advantageous alliances....

This, then, was one reason for making a closer alliance with England and France. The *second* reason was that England pledged herself to guarantee France's promises; of which the most important for Sweden was, not to begin a war in Germany. And it is a notable fact, that it was especially in response to England's persuasions and solicitations, and in order to obtain the friendship of so considerable a naval power, and *not* only out of consideration for France, that we entered upon the alliance. The *third* reason was that the alliance made no new stipulations, but merely confirmed those to which we were bound in terms of the peace of Westphalia.... The *fourth*, was that it by no means bound anybody to declare war, but reserved to us the right to mediate between all parties. The *fifth*, was that in virtue of an alliance which brought her 400,000 *riksdaler* a year, Sweden became a power to be reckoned with, and this without having to unsheath a single sword. And the *sixth* (which was the reason that Sweden had most in mind) was that this alliance was the only means which could hold back France from breaking the peace in Germany. . . .

. . . .

But although it is to be presumed that all this was sufficiently clear, it is nevertheless the case that various objections, of no small consequence, could be made to the French alliance. I present them here, and examine them one by one.

First objection. The first objection will no doubt be that Sweden interpreted the third clause in France's peace with the Emperor and Empire [at Westphalia] in a way which conflicted with the views of the other party to it. To which it is answered that there is no ground for the allegation, and that it is incapable of proof. For the alliance which the Emperor concluded with France in 1671 – long after the Peace of Westphalia – shows that the Emperor gave to the clause the same sense as that in which Sweden understood it. . . .

Second objection: that Sweden by making the alliance did undeniably desert the Triple Alliance. Anybody who argues on these lines can know very little of the matter; for England was of course the principal party to the Triple Alliance, and was nevertheless the power which invited Sweden to attack Holland. . . .

A third objection which might be brought against the French alliance, is that it was the real origin of the war; since in virtue of it Sweden was obliged to send troops to Germany, and it consequently happened that when no means of providing for them could be found, the resolution had to be taken to supply them from enemy country. This is indeed an extremely insidious argument, and may well mislead many persons unaware of the facts; but when it is properly examined, it turns out to be a myth, and an illogical one at that. For in the first place it is incontrovertible that Sweden would have been forced to send a considerable force to Germany even though no French alliance had existed. The whole of Germany was arming, as Denmark was also; and Sweden could hardly have sat still and looked on indifferently, but was bound to be nervous in case such a general conflagration, so close at hand, should spread to her own roof-tree.

. . . .

It is clear, therefore, that it was not Sweden's arming which was the cause of war with the Empire, but that the pretext for that war was taken from the rupture with Brandenburg which followed.

In the next place, nobody can reasonably contend that it was lack of supplies which led to our irruption into the Elector's territory: there were quite different, and much more important, reasons for what happened. For in the first place it was proved by reports which came in later that the troops would have been able to subsist in Pomerania and Bremen; and even though they might have been something of a burden to the country, that would have been preferable to the risk of total ruin. ... Secondly, if it had been only a question of supplies, they could have been found in the states of the Empire – in Mecklenburg, Saxe-Lauenburg, and other places adjacent to H.M.'s provinces – in return for subsequent payment out of the subsidies, if no better terms could have been had. And Count Bengt Oxenstierna, who was at that time H.M. envoy to the Emperor, can tell you that the Emperor and the states of the Empire would never have regarded such proceedings as a hostile act on Sweden's part, but would have been glad to agree to them.

But, finally, [there is the objection that] if the error lay in collecting a strong body of troops [in Germany] which it subsequently proved impossible to maintain, and if this was the reason which led us to resolve on a rupture, then it was all a French artifice, designed to produce just that result. To this it is answered that I raised this point in the Council at the time, but also reported the French Ambassador's own words, which were: 'if only you will be responsible for getting the troops across the sea, I will answer for their actions [when they get there]'; and this was taken into consideration. ...

. . . .

I come now to the second part of this paper, and to an accusation that has no less wide currency than the former; for there are many who have judged that *it was not so much the French Alliance as our untimely rupture with the Elector of Brandenburg, that was the cause of this war*, and that it was I who advised, consented to, and approved that rupture.

[Brandenburg, having attacked France as Holland's ally, proceeded to make peace with her through Swedish mediation; and Sweden at France's request gave an assurance that Brandenburg would henceforward keep out of the war. Brandenburg welcomed this, and concluded an alliance with Sweden on the basis of preserving the peace. But the Elector then proceeded to ally with Holland, and re-entered the war against France. Sweden remonstrated with Brandenburg; France remonstrated with Sweden.]

His Majesty had thus to consider, first, that France had a legitimate complaint at the ungrateful conduct of the Elector; next, that what the Elector was doing was in direct contradiction of the peace treaty between them. Further, that the affront which the Elector offered to Sweden by thus evading the terms of the alliance, was highly prejudicial to His Majesty's sovereign dignity. In the fourth place, that by such a rupture the Elector was once more kindling the flames of war in Germany. His Majesty was thus necessitated to declare himself ready to fulfil the terms of his alliance, if it should prove impossible to deflect the Elector from his purposes; and also was obliged to consider how to vindicate the honour of his crown. But all this was done with the qualification that His Majesty was anxious above all to use every means which could serve to avert any unpleasant complications....

With the coming of spring and the opening of the campaigning season of 1675, H.M. realized that there was no hope of an accommodation with the Elector; he was therefore forced to resolve upon more vigorous measures, and it was from these that the war with the Elector began....

. . . . . .

Since all that I have written has demonstrated that the causes of this war do not really lie in the French alliance, and that there were good grounds for the rupture with Brandenburg; as also that our plans were well and prudently conceived; the question may well suggest itself, how it was that our disasters occurred. It is certainly not incumbent upon me to offer an answer to this question; but I am prepared to satisfy a legitimate curiosity to the extent of avowing that I consider the prime cause to be the judgment of God's righteous wrath upon all those transgressions and sins which now prevail in our country, but especially upon that spirit of restless disrespect, which began to weary of peace and quietness, so that there was an almost general desire for war. This, I can fairly say, was the capital cause; and let us never believe that we have deserved any better of God than other lands and peoples who have had their periods of disaster.... God grant that our godlessness, and especially the atheism which is now rampant, the injustices which are practised, the avarice and unchristian usury, the oppression of the poor, the arrogance and pride of this Estate or that, the deceitfulness, and the abominable sly intrigues of a kind that the staunch and serious Swedes of former days never knew – God grant that these and other sins may not further kindle His anger, to consume what still remains of Sweden's former glory and prosperity.

DelaGardiska Archivet (ed. P. Wieselgren), vii, 48-54, 57-61, 76-7, 81, 83, 92-4

XLIII Foreign policy: new style, 1686

In the years after 1680 Karl XI solved the dilemma which had baffled the Regents. His aims were much the same as de la Gardie's; but he took care to provide himself with the means for realizing them. The reformed army once more became a first-class instrument of policy, as Karl XII's adversaries were to find. The rehabilitation of the royal finances, through the Reduction, by the fines on the ex-Regents, and at first also by heavy taxation, made Sweden independent of foreign subsidies. Karl was thus able to make a policy of neutrality credible, and to limit his commitments in accordance with his ability to discharge them: his reward was Sweden's mediation at Ryswick. Meanwhile he put up with what he could not help. For more than a generation Holstein-Gottorp had been a vital Swedish interest: not only from the dynastic connexion, but as an essential strategic link between Pomerania and Bremen, and a threat to Denmark's rear. But even here he would risk no action which was beyond his strength to make good. A victim of Louis XIV's *réunions*, he was one of the earliest members of William III's anti-French coalition, though he characteristically contrived to evade any serious exertion. He was conscious of the potential danger from Russia (§VI); but defence measures in the Baltic provinces had to be postponed to fortifications designed to protect Sweden proper from another Danish attack: he could not afford both. His achievement was to give Sweden independence of action, to cut his coat according to his cloth, to accept the logic of the altered international status of his country. The Proposition is a good example of his habit of taking the Diet into his confidence on great issues: their effective power might now be small, but he believed that he owed them honest explanations.

His Majesty's Secret Proposition to the Secret Committee of the Estates 15 September 1686

. . . .

First, as regards external affairs. It is true . . . that by the gracious aid and blessing of God, and by means of the cautious policies and diplomatic actions of H.M., the provinces and frontiers of this realm have so far been kept in peace; but it must be admitted . . . that the country, and H.M., have been exposed to more than one provocation and interference, which H.M. would most willingly have prevented or repulsed, if he had had the power to do so, and if there had not been a risk by doing so of becoming involved in war – a contingency which H.M. has sought to avoid by every means in his power, having regard to the present condition of the kingdom, and to the humble representations and desires of the Estates, as expressed at the last Diet. Dangers are now crowding upon us, and we can scarcely be secure from attacks which will have to be resisted by force if all else fails, and which at the best can be met only by negotiation under arms. What some of these dangers and difficulties are, H.M. will now briefly set forth.

I

It will not be unknown to you how the King of Denmark has possessed himself of the Duchy of Slesvig, and has not only deprived the Duke of Holstein of his sovereignty, rights and property in that Duchy, but has also so dealt with him in the Duchy of Holstein that the Duke has been forced to quit the country, and has lost his revenues and sustenance. This is a thing which concerns the honour and interest of H.M. and the Swedish crown. For the Duke of Holstein was comprehended in the peace of the North [*sc.* that of 1679], and H.M. is bound, both by the terms of that peace, and by particular engagements dating from his father's time (to say nothing of ties of blood), to secure restitution and guarantees for the Duke. It is indeed a major Swedish interest that the Duke should retain his lands and that Denmark be not strengthened by their acquisition, or the way be thus opened for an attack upon this country. The Duke now seeks the protection of H.M., and claims the benefit of our alliance and our promises. Nevertheless, H.M. has not been in a position to prevent the damage and insult which have been inflicted on him. H.M. did indeed try to induce the King of Denmark to forbear his designs, but without effect. By negotiation and treaties – as with the Emperor and the States-General – H.M. has endeavoured to persuade other powers to join with him in taking up the Duke's cause; and the Dukes of Brunswick have indeed shown themselves not unwilling. But on the one hand any such attempt has been hindered by France, as also by the Turkish war; and on the other hand our allies claim that the prime responsibility for taking action lies upon the Swedish crown, and that with this end in view the first step is to increase our forces in Pomerania and Bremen. . . . H.M. has indeed from time to time given hopes of doing something of the sort, in order to prevent our friends from detaching themselves from us; but lack of means, and the vulnerable position of those provinces, have made it impossible to take the measures which would be necessary for carrying through such a policy. Meanwhile the King of Denmark has gone further, and is reported actually to have attacked the town of Hamburg. This is an enterprise of far-reaching implications, which directly or indirectly affects H.M., and may entail very dangerous consequences; . . . for the whole Duchy of Bremen could be reckoned as lost, if any foreign power made itself master of Hamburg; and communications with Wismar and Pomerania would be cut off. . . .

II

Next, although H.M. is by inheritance the rightful owner of the Duchy of [Pfalz-]Zweibrücken . . . the financial stringency of the times has compelled him to suffer the aggression of the King of France upon this Duchy and its dependencies, under the pretext of a *réunion*; and by the Truce of Ratisbon France retains it in full sovereignty for the next twenty years. . . . As a result of these proceedings H.M. has up to this moment been kept out of the succession to his rights in the Duchy, and seems unlikely ever to be able to enjoy the usufruct, except upon terms which resemble total subjection.

III

The crown of Sweden is by public treaties recognized and pledged to be a guarantor of the peace of Westphalia. Numerous and grave violations of that peace, as well as of the peace of Nijmegen, have occurred in the last few years; especially the seizure by France of Strassburg, the whole of Alsace, etc., under various pretexts of their being *réunions*, dependencies, or necessary appendages. It is indeed the case that the Emperor and the Empire have been forced to accept a truce upon France's terms – a step which H.M. recognized to be their own affair, since he was in no position to do anything effective himself – but nevertheless France continues, in defiance of her pledged word, to make great alterations, imposed by force, in the civil and ecclesiastical arrangements of Strassburg, Alsace, and other places. In this matter H.M. has of course an identical and common interest with the Emperor and Empire; but also a particular interest of his own, inasmuch as he is one of the principal partners to, and guarantors of, the Westphalian settlement.

IV

Nor can His Majesty neglect to inform the Secret Committee of the dangers which seem to threaten the Protestant religion, which is subjected both in France and in Germany to violent persecutions. . . .

As to these four preceding points, it would seem to be pretty clear that they are hardly likely to be dealt with effectively merely by negotiation. But if the negotiation were backed by armaments, and if therefore our German provinces were put in such a posture of defence that any potential aggressor was forced to have second thoughts about aggression; and if, as a consequence of our arming, our friends and allies stuck together, so that we could speak with weight and authority – then it probably would be possible to do something about putting things right by way of negotiation, and we might also, as hitherto, avoid a war. It is therefore a matter of extreme importance that we should discuss and get some idea of how we are to find the means to strengthen our reserves of war-material, and to provide these provinces with sufficient troops. We must also not only bring the navy to a state in which it will be able to give better protection than in the past to the approaches, coasts and ports of this kingdom, but also to secure and utilize our sea-lanes to the German provinces: the safety of Sweden, after all, is mainly dependent on these overseas bastions, and we ought not to count the cost of maintaining the outworks, if it enables us to live secure and free from fear within our walls and bulwarks.

. . . .

VI

Although there seems to be a good chance that there will be no trouble from the side of Russia, since the peace with them has so recently been solemnly confirmed and sworn to – and especially in view of the fact that the Tsar has now concluded an alliance with Poland against the Tatars, which should keep him busy – still it should be said that at the last meeting on the frontier the Tsar's commissioners made very unreasonable attempts to secure rights of precedence and other diplomatic advantages over our own commissioners, especially during the preliminary discussions, and did indeed actually break off when our commissioners told them that they were not prepared to concede them. It is easy to see from this incident that if H.M. is ever to do business with that nation on a reasonable footing we shall have to make an imposing show of strength on that side, if we are to keep the negotiations going. . . .

Svenska ridderskaps och adels riksdagsprotokoll, xv, 142–8